FEAR NO EVIL

The 23rd Psalm

The Lord is my shepherd, I shall not be in want.
He makes me lie down in green pastures,
He leads me beside quiet waters,
He restores my soul.
He guides me in paths of righteousness
  for His name's sake.

Even though I walk through the valley
  of the shadow of death,
I will fear no evil, for You are with me;
Your rod and Your staff, they comfort me.

You prepare a table before me in the presence
  of my enemies.
You anoint my head with oil;
My cup overflows.
Surely goodness and love will follow me
  all the days of my life,
And I will dwell in the house of the Lord forever.

—from *The New International Version*

FEAR NO EVIL

USING THE 23RD PSALM

FOR HEALING AND SELF-RENEWAL

by Robert R. Leichtman, M.D.

ARIEL PRESS
Atlanta, Georgia

No royalties are paid on this book

This book was made possible by
a gift by Patricia Hamill
to the Publications Fund of Light

FEAR NO EVIL

ISBN 0-89804-037-X

Table of Contents

Preface

There are many ways to read a book. You will probably choose to read this one as I wrote it, from cover to cover. But your particular needs could also lead you to read it differently. To help facilitate your enjoyment of this book, therefore, I am including here a brief synopsis of each part and chapter.

Part I is an introduction to the general meaning and use of the 23rd Psalm.

Chapter 1 describes prayer as a tool for tapping our inner resources and potential strengths for healing, renewal, and personal growth.

Chapter 2 lays out the nature and purpose of prayer. This chapter is for those who have never learned, or have forgotten, the principles of prayer and the steps for developing effective techniques for prayer.

Chapter 3 delves into the arcane meaning of the symbols and metaphors of the 23rd Psalm. The language of this ancient prayer can obscure meaning if we fail to comprehend what each word and metaphor refers to in the context of our relationship with our Creator.

Chapter 4 provides an overview for the practical use

of this psalm to help us *connect* more fully with spiritual sources, *identify* more completely with our inner wisdom and strength, *heal and renew* ourself, and finally, *enrich* our understanding and *strengthen* our virtues of faith, joy, tolerance, patience, courage, and love.

Part II studies the meaning of each phrase of the 23rd Psalm. Each segment of the psalm invokes a particular spiritual quality or force which can be used to strengthen and vivify our individual efforts at prayer and meditation. A whole chapter—chapters 5 through 11—is devoted to each stanza.

Part III shows how the 23rd Psalm can be used to focus the energies of spirit into our field of consciousness, thereby integrating new life of spirit into our character. Chapter 12 explains how this work can be done.

In reading this book, keep in mind that it is possible for words to get in the way of understanding. This is true especially in the area of theology, where some people delight in splitting hairs and creating radical reinterpretations on the basis of a phrase here or there. The occasional phrase, taken out of context by an impassioned fanatic, can easily become a weapon. This has caused untold misery and completely unnecessary conflict in the history of religion.

In any scripture, it is the *whole* of the writing and its dominant themes which are significant. The details of traditions and scriptures are meant to add color and clarity to these general themes—not contradict them or become divisive points.

Therefore I will appeal to the reader's good sense to appreciate that God has many names, but one nature. There are many facets to this God, but, again, one nature. So also, there are many names for what Christians call the Christ, yet only one nature and quality to this power and wisdom. Despite this common sense view, facts and sensiblity have never stopped the arrogance or ignorance of the idolaters of scripture and tradition. Misguided fanatics of all ages and cultures have frequently taken something beautiful and sublime, twisted it with narrow misunderstanding, and used it as a weapon to intimidate and shame instead of lifting up and healing. These people and their organizations have done more to drive people away from God than virtually anything else, and we should reject their ideas and influence.

It should be clear that one name or label cannot contain the full definition or power of our Creator. It should make little difference whether we refer to our God as the Creator, Christ or Jesus, the Buddha, higher intelligence, higher power, the higher self, the infinite intelligence, or whatever. Like the proverbial rose, which is still as sweet and fragrant by *any* name, so also God is still powerful, wise, and loving by any name.

—*Robert R. Leichtman, M.D.*

Introduction

Anxiety and stress are common evils in most of our lives today. Unfortunately, the search for relief from these two intruders is usually frustrated. This lack of remedy is rarely due, however, to a shortage of solutions offered to us. The solutions are available—but are ignored, misunderstood, or misused.

Real solutions to life's most difficult problems are usually neither easy nor swiftly accomplished. They require knowledge, skill, effort, and self-discipline. Even more demanding is the fact that the answers and solutions we need often require us to confront the awesome truth about our self and our situation. In other words, we may have to admit that we do not have all the answers, that we have made some huge mistakes, that we have seriously misjudged people and events, and that we have often worked harder to keep our problems than we have worked to cure them.

This is why the masses consistently prefer comfortable illusions over the genuine effort to acquire the understanding and skills essential for the mature and spiritual life. Instead of facing the difficult task of growing in personal courage, we add to our problems the silent evil of escaping into passiveness. Instead of learning the exacting skill of being centered in our core strengths, we seek the subtle evil of learning to manipulate others. Instead of laboriously adding to our capacity for coping effectively with whatever lies before us, we prefer to learn the gentle evil of deflecting these responsibilities to others. Instead of seeking healing insights, we take shelter under mere platitudes.

Too often it seems that the truth that sets us free of anxiety and stress is not worth the price of the struggle involved in understanding or living it. And so, there is an eager reception for whatever is simple, effortless, and requires no sacrifice of resentments, fears, prejudice, or bad habits. The easy luxury of taking the path of least resistance leads to the ultimate evil of choosing comfort and security over the more difficult pursuit of health and growth of character. However, the stresses of unresolved conflict and unsolved problems remain. And so the struggle continues for effective solutions to our real problems.

Enduring comfort and healing power have always been available to everyone. They are not found in some exotic source, nor do we have to travel to a distant sacred place to acquire them. We do not even have to burn candles or incense! The most powerful source of comfort, guidance, power, and healing love is to be found in the deepest wellsprings of our self—*our spirit*.

It is not a new revelation to announce that we all have access to a power and intelligence greater than our personality—something we may call our soul, higher self, or our spirit. What is new to many is that we need *more than belief* in this concept to be effective in using this power and intelligence. The proper link to this power requires *knowledge and skill* as well as belief. We need greater knowledge to fully absorb the design and ways of spirit. We need greater skill to translate the patterns and principles of our spirit into the enlightened qualities and abilities that bring us healing and enrichment.

Fortunately, there are many ways of linking with the life of our spirit to help us find relief from stress and anxiety. There are, for instance, many prayers, meditations, invocations, and contemplations that are designed to help us in this way, as well as devotions, postures, and rituals.

Unfortunately, in times of stress, fatigue, and illness, we often need something simple, fast, and effective. This is the basic concept behind *Fear No Evil:* to provide a careful instruction in the profound meaning and practical use of the 23rd Psalm in helping us combat fear, anxiety, and distress.

As one of the oldest prayers in the Western religious tradition, this psalm has some automatic advantages over most other prayers. The specific benefits are many:

First, it is a well worn path of proven merit. It has, in the language of modern advertisers, thousands of satisfied customers who sing its praises.

Second, the individual phrases of this psalm, if properly understood, can be used as a form of mantra—words that invoke specific spiritual energies and blessings.

Third, using the 23rd Psalm with skill, intelligence, and devotion can strengthen our alignment to all the powers and qualities of our spiritual self. This, in turn, provides global and enduring benefits on all levels of our needs.

Fourth, the skillful use of this psalm assists us in flushing out discordant and immature qualities in our personality, such as persistent fears, doubts, and resentments that seem to return again and again to undermine our serenity.

Fifth, the proper use of this psalm can help us circulate new spiritual life and healing energies throughout our personality, leading to greater integration of our spirit and personality.

None of these results is possible, however, for those who merely "go through the motions" of saying this prayer. In fact, mindless repetition will produce no results at all, except the *illusion* that we have made an appeal to higher power. It will be necessary, instead, to summon considerable effort and imagination to dig under the common bland meanings of this prayer.

Effective prayer requires our conscious understanding combined with belief and the intent to enrich our personality. Therefore, I have provided a careful explanation of the symbolic meaning of each phrase. The language of the ancients is often poetic and rich in metaphor. The phrases and images suggested are designed to appeal to the most basic levels of our consciousness. The words and images are simple, and yet they convey very sophisticated concepts about our relationship to our Creator. This is why the proper and skillful use of the 23rd Psalm can be so effective in helping us to be comforted and supported by this benevolent power.

In practical terms, we can use the 23rd Psalm in many ways. We can use it as a source of emergency aid in times of crisis. Or we can use it as a way to break through wherever we have become stuck in our lives. We can use it as a source of courage when we feel overwhelmed in our ongoing struggles to cope with stressful situations. And we can use it as a daily ritual that helps re-center us in our strengths and deepen our conviction that God goes with us wherever circumstances take us each day.

The 23rd Psalm is a well worn and effective path to our inner life, and through this, all of the blessings of our Creator. Anything that can increase our understanding of how to use this path with greater effectiveness can produce countless benefits.

Fear No Evil
Part One

chapter 1

HOW THE 23rd PSALM
CAN HELP YOU

Everyone needs a little help occasionally. If we are fortunate, our friends will be there to aid us as we face the obstacles of life. But there can also be times when there seems to be little or no help. This may be because no one is available for us. At other times, it is because what others have to offer is not what we need.

The most difficult situations are those where only we can supply what we need to bolster our strength, confidence, and hope. Friends may offer reassurance or advice, but the hollow spot within us remains empty. All the external support we might receive then will not be enough to fill it. These are the times when we must find an *internal source* of guidance and strength to sustain us. Discovering and tapping these inner sources becomes a vital and urgent need for us.

This is when the use of effective prayer and meditation can be immensely valuable.

Prayer and meditation are old and well-proven tools for exploring and developing our inner resources and potential. They provide a highly effective means for evoking our inner wisdom, strength, hope, calmness and vitality. Each generation rediscovers the value and various techniques for using prayer in this manner. Fortunately, our spiritual traditions are rich in the varieties of prayer and meditation.

What is unfortunate, however, is that old things can get stale and arthritic unless renewed and revivified. This is certainly true of our techniques and practices of prayer and meditation. Prayer too easily becomes just a bunch of words mumbled quickly and mindlessly. Meditation often becomes just a passive state of pleasant restfulness. The real benefits of both are diminished or absent in such casual use.

The end result of the superficial use of prayer and meditation is unfortunate. Valuable tools for healing and support are broken and become unavailable to help us. By default, people then turn to others and groups in even more desperation for relief and support. This often merely adds an unwholesome dependency on top of their other problems. Even worse, many good people simply deteriorate into hopelessness, despair, and bitterness, because of their continuing unmet needs.

It is therefore important to restore the use of prayer and meditation to their full potential and benefits. This work is not as difficult as it may seem at first, because the old forms of prayer still retain all their value. It is we who, through ignorance and insensitivity, have forgotten how to use them correctly and effectively.

One of the great spiritual highways to the divine presence is the 23rd Psalm. It can be used for both prayer and meditation as a very powerful conduit to divine sources of healing, guidance, empowerment, and renewal.

What restores this "old war horse of prayer" for us is a greater understanding and appreciation of its inner structure and meaning.

Many of the ideas presented in this volume may seem, at first, to be strange—or even to contradict what you may have been taught. Please keep in mind that the best test for an idea or technique is *not* to judge it by our assumptions, traditions, or theories. What proves the validity and value of any idea is its usefulness to us—*not* how well it confirms our preferred beliefs. The one great principle that keeps us all honest and growing is the principle of spiritual pragmatism. This principle guides us by giving us a single primary standard for judging the value of any idea or technique. Simply stated, it says: *Judge by the results you get. What works, works. What doesn't work, doesn't!*

Ultimately, the primary goal of all prayer and meditation is to reconnect or deepen our connection with the best within us, which includes our divine potential. If this is achieved, all else—healing, renewal, and so on— becomes possible.

chapter 2

WHAT IS PRAYER AND WHY DO WE NEED IT?

Like any tool for helping us, there are effective and ineffective ways of using prayer. It is unfortunate that prayer is often practiced so poorly and ineffectively. Sometimes this is because too much religious baggage and associations have been attached to prayer. At other times, the tool of prayer is misused out of ignorance, misunderstanding, or laziness.

There are many reasons why we fail to make efficient use of prayer. The main ones are:

1. We do not understand the purpose of prayer.

2. We do not comprehend the nature of the power and intelligence that we invoke in prayer.

3. We do not understand our relationship with this power.

4. We do not know effective techniques for prayers.

The purpose of prayer

Prayer is a way to become better connected with a benevolent intelligence and power greater than our personality and body. We can use this connection to give thanks, to ask for help and guidance, or just to renew our confidence and self-control. Prayer is therefore a practical tool for helping ourself and others. It is a means to an end, not an end in itself.

The power and insights we invoke in prayer

The power invoked by prayer is mysteriously in and about us, available and responsive to our legitimate needs. Although we often fail to appreciate the fact of its support, this higher power is already a source of guidance, strength, and vitality which enables us to think, feel, move and express ourself. Through right belief, trust, and knowledge, we can increase our attunement to this power.

This benevolent, intelligent power has many names but one nature. It is universal and available to anyone. Since it is *benevolent,* it is a friendly power—not remote, uncaring, or vengeful. Since it is *intelligent,* it knows us and our legitimate needs better than we, as a personality, do. Since it is *powerful,* it is greater than any sickness, fear, doubt, or other problem we have. Since it is *eternal,* it can outlast our resistance and rebellion against its authority and laws—and even our denial of its influence. It has a plan and design for our mature character and self-expression. It also cares about us enough to overrule our requests for help when they conflict with our divine design for maturity and mature behavior. And since it is *indwelling* in our being, it constitutes the essence of our human and suprahuman potential.

For all these reasons, this indwelling intelligence should be regarded as a very powerful resource for us. That is, our inner, spiritual life is a source of many useful things:

• Intelligent guidance to help us make good decisions, solve problems, and heal confusion.

• Love, to help us be more forgiving and tolerant so we can heal resentments.

• Joy, to be more cheerful and optimistic and heal despair.

• Power, to add strength to our courage and heal fear.

• Vitality, to renew and heal us.

Our relationship to divine power

Prayer is not reserved for use only by the pious and devoutly religious. We do not have to be a "good" person to pray. Neither do we have to approach prayer in a state of guilt, contrition, or self-rejection. While religion is designed to help us relate to the creative and spiritual forces of life, it often gets in the way of enlightened living and growth. Rigid rules and expectations, narrow beliefs and proscriptions more often inhibit access to our inner healing life than liberate it.

If we return to the basics of prayer, we will find that it is a pragmatic effort to work with a power and intelligence within us which is greater than the body or personality. This means we need to regard this benevolent power as a friend—not a mean-spirited force that is eager to punish us and otherwise make us miserable.

As a friend, this power will support our worthwhile activities and needs. Also as a friend, it will not support behaviors that are destructive and immature. In short, this higher power is benevolent without being permissive. Likewise, it is intelligent without being indifferent to our indiscretions.

Because this power is indwelling, it is always available. If we have difficulty contacting it, it is probably because our personality is in turmoil or in such a dark mood that we are effectively disconnected from the more subtle realms where spirit can be reached. For instance, if we are drowning in an overload of physical sensations and hurt feelings, we become relatively earthbound. This state of mind disengages us from the levels of awareness where we can find guidance, insight, peace, love and strength. Therefore, it is important to make the appropriate changes in ourself to reestablish this connection in consciousness.

Because this power is universal, it is governed by certain principles or laws. These laws are invisible and operate completely without our awareness or approval. Being quite independent of our preference, they cannot be revoked or denied by our wishes or demands. Just as gravity works on the physical plane whether we believe in it or not, similar laws operate to govern right human relationships and our relationship to higher powers.

As they influence us, these universal laws act as *incentives* to encourage us to think and behave maturely. One such law, stated in its popular form, tells us that we should love one another. If we translate this into human behavior, it means we need to conduct ourself in thought and deed with charity and generosity. By living in conformity with these laws, the universe also becomes more charitable and generous toward us, which is the incentive to us for obeying them.

These same laws likewise provide *disincentives* to correct and discipline behavior that is not in harmony with our design for maturity and enlightenment. Thus, if we act with selfishness and malice, we are creating disharmony between us and our world. As a direct consequence of this behavior, the universe will be unable to treat us generously. Therefore, we will automatically begin to bear the unpleasant consequences of selfishness in our personal world. In this way, universal law discourages, through disincentives, immature behavior.

All of this makes our relationship with this higher and benevolent power somewhat complex—which is appropriate, since the alliance is meant to be rich and pervasive. It cannot be reduced to a few simple rules, nor can it be forged entirely out of faith or devotion. It is *the intelligent use* of faith and love—not ignorant fanaticism, superstition, or mindless devotion—that makes this relationship come alive and become one of intelligent collaboration.

Because this relationship is complex, one important key to developing and strengthening this connection is to be mindful that *this power is our friend*—a very powerful, wise, and benevolent patron. Making this power our patron and friend helps eliminate the common tendency to idolize our divine possibilities to the point where they seem remote and are not achieveable. We would be comfortable seeking a friend for advice; we would not be intimidated by a friend, nor by his counsel. We can admire a friend and will use him or her as a model for our attitudes and behavior. And we will be interested in keeping the relationship thriving with our affectionate concern, loyalty, and cooperation.

We have nothing to fear from a loyal friend. A good friend will not be jealous but will take delight in our success. A friend will want to help us be successful, healthy, and fulfilled. So also, a good friend may, from time to time, criticize us or warn us about what we have said or done or are about to do. Friends do not let friends go unwarned about their mistakes or indiscretions, because they want to spare them the harsh consequences of those mistakes. Such warnings and criticisms are motivated by good intentions and goodwill. Again, we have nothing to be afraid of in a true friend.

This is the general tone of a healthy and cooperative relationship with the great benevolent power that dwells within us and pervades the universe. It supports us and helps us like a good friend.

In order to pray intelligently, we must learn to approach this great friend accordingly.

Effective techniques for prayer

The most popular explanation of effective prayer is

that you simply "talk to God." If this definition sounds a bit too simple, it is because it is! If our human nature is complex and our relationship to higher power is even more complex, it is unlikely that such a simple connection would be sufficient to harness all the benefits of prayer. If someone were to tell us that all there is to violin playing is to hold the violin in our left hand and use our right hand to scrape the bow over the strings of the violin, we would ignore him as simpleminded. Just so, we should ignore simplistic instruction about prayer.

One of the first mistakes often made in the effort to pray effectively is that many people assume that prayer is a quiet and passive state where we ask God for a blessing, then wait for it to occur. If nothing happens, we are supposed to assume we did not deserve this blessing— or that God does not want us to have it.

But effective prayer is not just the act of passively asking for something. The purpose of prayer is to reconnect and start cooperating more fully with higher power. This means we need to collaborate with this higher power, not just idolize it and then passively wait for the magic to happen while we just "observe" and "keep the faith."

Effective prayer is a skill—not "just something we do." It involves more than just bowing our head and mumbling words. There are four simple steps in effective prayer. Each is essential but easy to perform. They are:

1. Preparation.
2. Attunement.

3. Invocation.

4. Response.

Step one: Preparation. We take time to quiet and center ourself in the certain belief that we have a good relationship with our Creator and seek Its advice and support.

Step two: Attunement. We adopt a state of mind and feeling of genuine humility. Real humility has nothing to do with groveling, shame, or self-rejection. Genuine humility is simply the recognition that there truly is a power and intelligence greater than ourself, and we want to know it better and follow it in so far as possible. This kind of humility requires us to be as alert and responsive as possible—not dulled by deep mindlessness and emptiness. It heightens our alertness, curiosity, and devotion. As a result, we become willing to subordinate our thinking to a wisdom greater than ours, our feelings to a love and joy greater than ours, and our will to a purpose and authority greater than ours.

For emotional people, humility is most easily practiced on the wavelength of reverence, devotion, and a grateful mindfulness of higher possibilities.

For more intellectual individuals, humility is practiced as trust, a positive expectancy toward life, and an acceptance of the fact of a higher power and a spiritual design for our life.

For the strong-willed, humility is best achieved by dedication to noble purpose and higher authority, a commitment to cooperate and serve this higher purpose, and a determination to impose this higher purpose on ourself and our self-expression.

Step three: Invocation. We generate a tension between who we are as a personality and our higher possibilities. This tension is something we create by our hopes, aspirations, dedication to noble ideas, and our faith in all of our divine possibilities. This yearning and positive belief is what summons or attracts higher power to us for communion. Through this connection we can strengthen and enrich ourself as a new down-pouring of divine blessings moves into us.

Step four: Response. We do more than just passively and subjectively "feel good" about this experience. We truly engage in our part of the collaboration by seeking *to comprehend and internalize* the new insights, love, joy, courage, values, priorities, and vitality that come to us as a result of our invocations. In practical terms, this means we become intent on adding new wisdom, love, and courage to the mainstream of our beliefs, values, and expectations. In this manner, new healing and enriching life can be grounded in the very structure of our character and habits of self-expression.

One of the key disappointments of those who pray is that they often seem to get no answer to their prayers. They may be overlooking the possibility that they have already had their prayers answered—by having sufficient intelligence to solve their own problems, enough love to do their own forgiving, enough enthusiasm to start a new project, enough power to complete current work, and enough knowledge and vitality to do their own healing.

People forget that, since higher power resides in us—as our full potential for wisdom, love, joy, creativity, and vitality—spirit often has done its portion of the "work" long before we get around to asking for help. Often, we are like the well-tuned violin waiting for the master's touch. The violin is ready to provide music; there is nothing more it must do. The violin is comparable to our own endowment of real and potential wisdom, talent, love, joy, and all the other fruits of spirit. They are ready to help us long before we think to utter a prayer. It is we who must "lift our bow and stroke the strings" to activate the potential of this instrument.

It is in this manner that we participate actively and intelligently in collaborating with the life of spirit so that we can ground what we invoke from spirit in our character and body, as an enlightened consciousness and self-expression.

This is why we pray.

chapter 3

SYMBOLISM

IN THE 23rd PSALM

Nothing destroys our understanding of archetypal symbols more quickly than the careless or ignorant translation of these symbols into words or concepts. Words can soothe or hurt, reveal or confuse, and complicate or simplify. The right choice of words can illuminate or beguile, depending on how well we comprehend their significance. Words frequently get in the way of understanding, unless we make the effort to comprehend what they mean in terms of their dictionary definition, the context in which they are used, and the general purpose they are designed to serve.

Because words are only *vehicles for meaning*, those who wish to convey complex ideas often use word pictures and metaphors. The more poetic language of word pictures and metaphors has the advantage of transcending the difficulty in translating intricate concepts to people of differing cultures and languages. In addition, metaphors and word pictures easily convey the drama and color of complex ideas in ways that transcend mere words; they can even communicate directly with our unconscious.

The unique language and symbols of the 23rd Psalm merit a few words of explanation. There are two important reasons for this: first, understanding strengthens our faith; and second, the more we understand something, the more we can make good use of it, whether it is a machine, a technique, or a philosophical concept.

The 23rd Psalm opens by comparing God—"Our Lord"—to a herder of sheep, implying that we are the good sheep who are guided, protected, and sustained by this divine shepherd. What modern city dwellers may not appreciate is the fact that sheep are among the most helpless of farm animals; they need a lot of human guidance or they will become lost, starved, or diseased. Sheep are very timid and easily panic; they often run blindly in their fright and get lost or fall into holes where they cannot get out. When sheep have a full coat of wool, their center of gravity shifts to a higher level. Therefore, a simple fall can be most dangerous, because they often just roll over on their backs and cannot get up. They may simply lie helplessly in this position until they starve or are killed by predators.

Sheep are very shy, herd animals. They will stay in one spot and eat the grass down to the roots and destroy it, unless they are led to fresh pasture by the shepherd. They will drink polluted or stagnant water unless the shepherd leads them to fresh sources.

Sheep are also prone to being irritated by flies and

ticks, and the shepherd must apply an oily insect repellent or the sheep can become so upset that they stop eating. The pregnant ones may have miscarriages. Anointing sheep with these soothing oils is done with considerable frequency to keep them comfortable.

In ancient as well as modern times, sheep are put out to pasture during the warm months. These are times when various kinds of predators look to the sheep for a quick meal. The ancient shepherds always carried two tools: a staff and a rod. The **rod** was usually spiked with sharply pointed nails, so that it would inflict maximum damage to anything it hit. The shepherd often had to use it to beat off dogs or wolves or other predators that easily could devastate a flock in a few days. Thus the rod became a symbol of the power of the shepherd to protect the herd and ward off its enemies.

The **staff** was the other major tool of the shepherd. This is a tall "walking stick" with a curved top. The shepherd used the incurved top end (the crook) to lift sheep out of holes in the ground where they might have gotten stuck. They also used the staff to lift newborn lambs to place them close to their mother, because using their hands could easily leave a foreign human scent that might cause the mother to reject their own newborn.

Because of this usage, the staff became a symbol of the power of God to support and sustain us. It also became the model for the bishop's staff or crozier.

The ancient Egyptians used similar symbols and tools.

Many statues and drawings of ancient pharaohs show them holding a *crook and a flail* in their crossed arms. These are the counterparts of the staff and the rod, and in their culture, they represent similar qualities: the crook symbolizes the power to bless and support; The flail symbolizes the power to discipline and punish.

Every spring, the shepherd drives his flock from their winter pens out to the pastures in the high hills or plateaus. Sheep are not good travelers, so the shepherd usually scouts the land to find the easiest passage up the hills or mountains to the high pastures. This almost always means going up the low, easy passage of the valleys. These avenues provide the most level ground plus the most likely place to find water to drink and vegetation to eat on this migration.

Unfortunately, the valleys are also dangerous to the sheep, because they are highly exposed to predators at this time. Predators can lurk behind rocks and shrubs and then attack swiftly before the sheep can run or the shepherd defend his flock. Therefore, passage through these valleys foreshadows the possibility of swift death for the sheep.

Consequently, these valleys came to symbolize any form of danger or threat to our well-being in our movement through the whole of our physical life.

The second major set of symbols in the 23rd Psalm concerns the image of a table of food or banquet set for us by a generous host. This too can be interpreted in terms of the shepherd and his flock. It can also be viewed in more directly human terms as symbolic of being the dinner guest of a wealthy host.

If we choose to interpret the symbology of the "banquet" or "table" prepared for us as referring to sheep, then the table becomes the rich pasture found in the high plateaus at springtime. Since the predators of the sheep are still hanging about, this pasture is certainly "in the presence of enemies"—wolves, dogs, and so on.

Possibly a better interpretation of this symbol of the banquet "table prepared in the presence of our enemies" is the suggestion of being the guest of a wealthy and generous host who richly provides room and food for us. In ancient times, travelers had few and only rather primitive inns to use as temporary accommodations. Far more desirable, if it could be arranged, was to be welcomed as a guest by some local landowner. The code of the host in that day was far more complex and carried more responsibility. A guest, once accepted, was treated almost like family. Enemies of the guest were expected to honor the code of hospitality and set aside any feud until the guest left the house of the host.

Therefore, the symbology of the banquet table being prepared for us suggests the divine blessing and heritage we all have as children of a very rich and generous God. In this context, the "enemies" can mean traditional *external* threats of any kind, human or otherwise. As a metaphor, however, the word "enemies" can also refer to our *internal* adversaries, as they emerge from the dark side of our character—the self-sabotaging qualities of our own anger, pessimism, fear, anxiety, or doubts.

The final part of the 23rd Psalm speaks of "dwelling in the house of the Lord forever." Certainly, a specific and concrete building of bricks and mortar is not implied. Rather, it refers to a figurative house—our spiritual body, the "house not made with hands." If we accept that the "banquet" symbolizes the real and potential strengths that we have in our innate spiritual nature, then the house of the Lord is our *eternal and divine host*. In other words, the house of the Lord is a poetic phrase or symbol for our spiritual home or the Kingdom of God within us. It is meant to be "the home" or center of our spiritual and permanent individuality—a center to which we return over and over for renewal, healing, and new blessings.

Returning to our spiritual center or core is one of the primary uses of effective prayer. The 23rd Psalm makes it clear in poetic language that we cannot only *return* to this source, but that we can dwell or *stay in the awareness of* our divine heritage of wisdom, love, and strength at all times.

If we study and contemplate the use of the words and symbols of the 23rd Psalm in this manner, we will have powerful fuel for thought. Careful reflection on the meaning and relevance of these complex ideas can do much to open up our awareness to noble possibilities and activate our higher potential.

This is the promise of the 23rd Psalm.

chapter 4

HOW TO USE
THE 23rd PSALM

The 23rd Psalm is rich with meaning and has the power to evoke most if not all of our inner human and divine strengths and potentials. Like any tool, the more we know how to tap the many benefits and uses of the 23rd Psalm, the more we can apply them to our needs.

Unfortunately, some people pray with a very limited understanding and expectations. Many never even question the adequacy of their understanding of why they pray or the effectiveness of their techniques for praying. As a result, they miss many good opportunities to deepen their relationship with God and all of their divine possibilities.

It is useful, therefore, to highlight the potential applications of the 23rd Psalm when used as a prayer and invocation to divine qualities. More specifically, this psalm can be used for:

1. Enriching our connection to our divine source.
2. Centering in our strengths, wisdom, and talents. This includes becoming more *detached* from outer problems and more *empowered* by a closer

identification with our core strengths and inner potential.

3. Aiding in cleansing and healing ourself of negative qualities while bringing in new vitality.

4. Enhancing our understanding, courage, faith, patience, goodwill, tolerance, and all other fruits of the spirit. This includes enriching our belief that we are a well-loved child of a powerful Creator who supports us in all our worthwhile struggles.

If we use the phrases and symbols of the 23rd Psalm as seed thoughts for our prayerful reflection, this great psalm can be a powerful resource for us. A mere intellectual review of these ideas is of little value, however. The serious student of spirit and psychology must be prepared to reflect deeply on these suggested interpretations, and "try them out" in prayer and meditation. This will aid in achieving a deeper realization of the power and meaning of these concepts.

In other words, I can only present here a *recipe* for gathering insights and new healing life. Each reader will have to seek the *ingredients* of spiritual health in his or her own divine possibilities.

The first part of this psalm improves our **connection with God**. *"The Lord is my shepherd"* indicates a Creator who is very "shepherding" toward us—caring, protective, concerned, and ready to guide us, not scornful or punitive. By dwelling on the meaning and significance of this concept of a caring and benevolent God, we are encouraged to believe, trust, and accept this higher power. This strengthens our relationship to God.

Centering begins with the phrase, *"He makes me lie down in green pastures."* Drawing from the metaphor of sheep, "green pastures" symbolize nourishment and sustenance for us as well as an abundance of all good things in general. As our thoughts move in this direction, we become more focused or centered in our core strengths of character: our real and potential qualities, talents, knowledge, and spiritual resources.

Part of centering also includes becoming more calm. And so the psalm continues: *"He leads me beside quiet waters."* "Quiet waters" is a symbol for calm, unruffled, and clear emotions. As we cultivate serenity, we are more able to mobilize and utilize our common sense, patience, and tolerance, instead of gyrating from our immediate, strong reactions to events, past or present.

All of these changes nurture our ability to center in our higher human nature and spiritual self so we can view and respond to our life situation with serenity, dignity, and strength.

Cleansing and healing are fostered by the 23rd Psalm in several ways. Just by drawing closer to the source of our life—our spirit—we bring new healing vitality into our minds and hearts and bodies. Just as we become warmer by sitting closer to a fire, so also we become revitalized and lifted up in our mood and thinking as we move closer in awareness to our inner wisdom, love, joy, courage, and peace.

Beyond this, however, are the powerful energies

evoked by the stanza referring to the passage of sheep through "the valley of the shadow of death." Here is where the shepherd's rod and staff can comfort us. The *rod* is the divine power to dispel or fight off enemies from without or within. This is significant, as we all eventually come to recognize our worst enemies are often our own fears, resentments, doubts, jealousies, despair, or guilt. The power of our Creator works as a cleansing and healing force as we use it to dispel these personal demons, by cleansing us of some degree of these qualities.

Likewise, the *staff* is the divine power to bless and increase all good and noble qualities in us. The direct healing benefits of extra love, joy, patience, endurance, or wisdom can be enormous.

In addition we are told that we need not fear evil (any threat or danger) because the shepherd is with us (not remote or unavailable to us). As we appreciate and deepen our understanding of what this means, we are reminded that the great benevolent power of our Creator is with us in all of our struggles. This aids in healing our sense of alienation and hopelessness.

The final major benefit of using the 23rd Psalm is for **enrichment** of our knowledge, faith, empowerment, vitality, and joy. This benefit is embodied throughout the entire psalm, but it is specifically stressed in the last half. It relates that the Creator has prepared "a table before me in the presence of my enemies." Once more "enemies" is a reference to *any* of our problems, illnesses, struggles, and suffering. This psalm equates our God to a generous and wealthy host who is pleased to present us with an abundance of qualities to nourish our character and our needs for guidance, encouragement, confidence, healing, opportunity, and sustaining power. We are told these blessings pour out in unlimited amounts, to the point where "our cup"—our ability to receive—is filled to overflowing.

Finally, we are told that "goodness and love"—God's blessings and mercy—will be with us forever and that we will dwell forever in the "house of the Lord," a higher conscious state characterized by confidence, serenity, insight, faith, and hope. What could be more uplifting and enriching to our minds and hearts than this realization?

Even when interpreted on a fairly literal, "exoteric" level, it is obvious that the 23rd Psalm is a hymn of great power and meaning. It is a vehicle which can bring the light and presence of God's Life into our own—to cast out doubts, defeat worry, and conquer evil.

Yet this is not the whole story of the 23rd Psalm, for this is a song of great subtlety and many levels of inner meaning. It is one of those unique statements about divine life that can never be worn out or exhausted by too much use.

The hidden meanings of the 23rd Psalm will be explored in Part II, stanza by stanza, with each verse being considered in a chapter by itself.

Fear No Evil
Part Two

chapter 5

THE LORD IS MY SHEPHERD, I SHALL NOT BE IN WANT

The Theme

The first lines of the 23rd Psalm declare for us two vital spiritual principles. The first statement reveals the nature of our God. The second announces the character of our relationship to God.

Since God is like a shepherd to us, our Creator is an intelligent and benevolent power Who cares for us. In unambiguous terms, we are told that we have a God who cares about us and works to protect, guide, and preserve our life.

The tone of our relationship to God is, therefore, that of someone who is well loved, protected, guided, and supported by a power and intelligence greater than ourself. As we come to understand and appreciate the quality of this relationship, we are comforted. We can then live in the continuous faith that we have access to divine assistance in times of trouble and temptation. This means we can call on strengths, creative ideas, healing love, and vitality greater than we can supply out of our human capacities and personal efforts. In this way, we come to know that "we shall not be in want."

The Meaning of the Symbols

The shepherd of a flock of sheep is like a god to the sheep, in that the shepherd is vastly more wise, capable, and powerful. This brief analogy tells us a great amount about the nature of our God.

The shepherd has vision—the vision to find new and better pastures, recognize dangerous plants, scout for water supplies, and find lost sheep. So also, our Creator has a vision of all the wonderful potential in us—the greatness we can become. Our Creator guides us away from dangers and temptations, toward our opportunities.

The shepherd has knowledge and skills to help his sheep at times of illness and birth. He has the capacity to help heal the sheep at times of injury and infections. Our Creator likewise provides guidance and healing vitality to us—directly as an acceleration of our innate healing mechanism and indirectly through external agents of healing.

The shepherd has the power to ward off dangerous predators and the power to preserve and promote the well-being of sheep in many other ways. He is always there for them. So also, our Creator provides the power to establish justice and repel discordant forces. More importantly, our Creator has the power to bless and enrich our life and character with love, joy, wisdom, talent, and grace. And since God dwells within us as the very essence of our existence, divine forces are always with us. We too are supported and protected by a great benevolent power.

Relating these symbols to our human condition

What this passage informs us about God is basic to the whole message of this psalm. We are being told that our God is concerned about our needs and is ready to provide personal direction and support for us. Like the sheep of a flock, we can rely on the guidance and protection of our Creator. Just as the shepherd is there to make certain that the sheep will have food, water, and protection, so also we have a caring God who works to be certain that our basic needs (not necessarily all our personal wants) will be secured. Just as the shepherd is there to anoint the cuts and insect bites of sheep with soothing oil, so also we are anointed (blessed) with the reassurances and strength that comfort us.

This does not mean that we have no responsibility for our welfare and survival—just that we have a guarantee that support will be there when we cannot completely supply it by our own efforts.

This concept that the Lord God is our shepherd actively rejects the false belief of a distant or punitive God who is full of wrath and sends down punishment to us. If we relate to our Creator as sheep relate to their shepherd, the clear implication is that we, like sheep, might become lost and forget about our divine purpose and resources. However, our shepherding God *will go after us to rescue us* as necessary. In other words, we are not punished and exiled for our mistakes; rather, the mistakes themselves punish us as we stray from our proper path of decision and effort. Like wayward sheep, our

Creator guides and corrects us and brings us back into the flock—our place in life—where we belong.

The opening lines of the 23rd Psalm spell out the fact that we are to have a personal relationship with God. In other words, our Creator is both a universal power and intelligence and also a personal benefactor to us. In the poetic terms of this psalm, our God is a very shepherding God who considers each of us important and thus cares for us by guiding, protecting, and sustaining our needs. Later on in this psalm, we are told that this shepherding God is "with us" to help support and protect us. This reference reconfirms the concept of a warm and personal relationship to our God.

The Spiritual Qualities and Insights Invoked

There are three major insights to be gleaned from these opening lines:

1. The comfort of knowing that we belong to something powerful and kind. We are never alone, even though it may seem that we have been abandoned or rejected. We have an internal connection to intangible powers which can provide tangible support.

2. The comfort of knowing that a benevolent authority goes before us to make our life more safe, secure, and productive. The power of divine order and our innate divine design is always present to direct us and help us regulate our life. The signs and agents of this invisible support will be visible to us.

3. The comfort of knowing we are protected and will

be helped in times of trouble. When we feel lost in the confusing situations of our life, rescuing forces and opportunities are sent to assist us. While this help rarely arrives in the form of a shepherd, it will emerge inside of us or about us when it is needed.

Increasing Our Response to These Qualities

The most important thing we can do to prepare to discover and embrace God's benevolent guidance and support is to practice enlightened humility. Enlightened humility is our ability to appreciate the fact that there is a great benevolent intelligence and authority available to us. This appreciation must be translated into a willingness to share our thoughts, feelings, motives, and beliefs with a power and intelligence greater than ourself. This means cultivating a devoted belief, reverent trust, and willing acceptance of this higher power.

Nowhere in the practice of enlightened humility is there any hint of becoming a mindless, empty person devoid of thought or initiative. What is implied is that we need to act in a conscious, intelligent, and active way to follow the plan and design of a more powerful, benevolent, and wise authority. It is cooperation and collaboration that is needed—not coma and emptiness!

The intelligent practice of humility in this context means two things. First, we need to consciously seek to understand God's nature and plan for us—His purpose, qualities, plans, and laws—rather than unconsciously seek it through using only our emotions—our faith and belief.

Belief alone or belief that we can learn or should learn is not enough. It will not accomplish the task of working with our divine plan any more than merely sitting down at a piano and believing we can play it actually means that we can do it. Knowledge and skill are also required for achievement in both instances. We need to actively pursue the study and understanding of our divine nature and its design for us. In addition, we need to learn how to express this more fully in our character and lifestyle.

Second, we need to share our life with our divine nature, by adapting our thinking, attitudes, and behavior to be in greater harmony with our divine design and purpose. Sharing means that we are to help one another. Sharing with God is often misunderstood to mean that God gives us what we want and then we accept it gratefully. It actually means that God helps us by providing *the seed* of great ideas to guide us, *the seed* of noble qualities to enrich us, and *the strength* to use them. In return, we help God by accepting these blessings and honoring our duty to follow our divine plan towards wholeness. As this transformation occurs, we continue to help God by contributing to the larger work of spiritualizing our culture and civilization.

In this sense, sharing involves an active and intelligent collaboration leading to a progressive enlightenment of our character and lifestyle. Hard and honest work—not wishing and hope—are essential for this achievement.

Unfortunately, many people substitute something less than this in their effort to relate to their divine Creator. Far too many people diminish or destroy their hope for divine support in one of three simple and frequently practiced ways.

The first way we commonly sabotage our relationship to God is by substituting self-absorption for enlightened humility. This is demonstrated in those who are so immersed in their hurts, losses, problems, suffering, and fears that they leave no room in their hearts or minds for divine possibilities. Bogged down in their current feelings of fear, anger, guilt, doubt or despair, these people try to pray and relate to God on this impoverished wavelength. Surrounded by the darkness of their misery, they hope for magical relief but tend to stay anchored in their own suffering. For them, the darkness of their suffering often remains unbroken.

With enlightened humility we are able to act with confidence and hope, inspired by the shepherding power and love of our Creator—not by our regrets about our wants, hurts, or wounds. This humility continues with the belief that we are endowed with God's blessings from the beginning, and that we are honored with a divine power that will seek to protect and preserve our life.

The second way we diminish our connection to God is by making God remote and virtually inaccessible. This is widely and commonly achieved by idolizing God to the point where we make the divine presence distant and untouchable while decreasing our own significance toward zero! Some people are so busy trying to surrender to God and become empty, devoid of thought, and "transparent" to divine direction that they *disconnect* their capacity to receive and retain divine blessings. In scriptural terms, they are dedicated to becoming the loyal slave to God, devoid of any independent thought or initiative. In psychological terms, they are making the erroneous assumption that emptiness is the best preparation for wisdom and maturity.

With enlightened humility we strive to meet God, not with our emptiness, but at our point of need and our full capacity to utilize new life of spirit. Instead of attempting to meet divine wisdom with a "transparent mind," we must greet it with an *alert mind*, which is prepared to translate divine guidance into useful plans and practical solutions for whatever challenges us. The intent is to work with God to bring divine qualities inside us and to invest them in our self-expression—not merely adore a deity who remains remote and unavailable.

The third and most difficult-to-recognize way we diminish our connection with God is to substitute sanctimony, rigid convictions, and righteous beliefs in traditions for intelligent humility. Some people easily turn common religious practices into a *barrier* rather than a *bridge* to spirit. They let the formal rules of religious practices get in the way of the presence of spirit and its power to enrich us.

It is, therefore, very appropriate to return to the opening lines of the 23rd Psalm for the key to a healthy and meaningful relationship to God. These lines remind us that our God is *a living presence* of wisdom, benevolence, and dynamic strength—not just a pile of rules and dogma. These same statements also help us understand that our God is a personal force, who considers us important and who cares about us.

Without this basic understanding, the rest of the significance and benefits of using the 23rd Psalm may be lost.

Therefore, the metaphor of the good shepherd and his flock sets the tone of our link with God. The ideal keynotes of our relationship to our Creator are devotion, respect, trust, and dedication to its authority and love for us. We are to be friends with God, not slaves. Our role in this friendship is to translate the guidance and blessings of this friend into our mature character and self-expression.

As we practice enlightened humility and accept a personal relationship with our God, we start to feel comforted and confident that, with God, we can endure!

Using This Stanza for Healing and Growth

There are three main "ills" this passage can help us heal:

1. *Aloneness*. The fear of being rejected and abandoned can cripple our ability to defend ourself and survive our challenges. When our situation seems to overwhelm us and we feel isolated and alone in our struggles,

it is marvelously reassuring to know that a higher power cares for us very deeply. When it seems that our world has rejected us, the conviction that our shepherding Creator still cares for us can be the one light that relieves the darkness about us.

2. *Uncertainty.* The fear of the unknown often frightens us more than any terror known to us. When it seems that the very foundations of our world have fallen apart, we become unsure about what to do—as well as who we are. It is comforting to know that a power greater than anything in our world stands ready to help us bring order out of chaos.

3. *Anxiety.* The fear of threatening events and forces can paralyze our ability to protect ourself and preserve what we have. It is reassuring to know that the protecting power of our Creator is with us always in our hour of need.

Summary

The whole of the 23rd Psalm is excellent for anyone who needs help in times of personal struggle. The special value of these two opening statements is to connect us with this great benevolent power and deepen our understanding that God is a powerful friend and reliable guide at all times. As we come to appreciate and respond to this power, we will experience a sense of calmness and confidence sweeping through us. This is because we know, deep in our hearts and minds, that we are never alone or without guidance and support. It is only the distraction of our outer struggles and frustrations that, sometimes, makes it seem that we are alone and abandoned.

Study Guide

1. What is my belief about the nature of God? Do I conceive of God as largely unknowable, or as knowable in part? As remote or near? As being outside or within myself? As a potential threat or as a friend? As uncaring or as understanding my needs?

2. What kind of relationship do I have with God? Is there respect and acceptance or just fear and intimidation? How often is this relationship contaminated with guilt, resentment, doubt, and self-rejection? How often do I notice my divine blessings? How often am I grateful for them?

3. How do I exercise or practice this relationship? Am I willing to subordinate my thinking and purpose to God's direction and insight? Do I expect to be able to preserve my resentments and assumed limitations while having a good relationship with God? What am I willing to give up in the way of blame, anger, fear, doubts, illness, and stubbornness to enrich my personal relationship to God?

4. Am I able to distinguish what I need from what I wish I could have? Would a loving and intelligent God give me everything I wished for? Do I completely understand that my highest good might well be different from what I currently prefer?

5. What do I expect out of my relationship with God? That I will magically be spared difficulty and hardship, or that I will be given the guidance and strength to overcome them? That I will have all problems solved and all burdens lifted, or that I will be supported *as I exercise* my personal responsibility and initiative in working out these things?

chapter 6

HE MAKES ME LIE DOWN IN GREEN PASTURES, HE LEADS ME BESIDE QUIET WATERS.

The Theme

Having established a trusting and responsive relationship with God, the 23rd Psalm now continues with a description of how God will help us. The theme of this stanza is that God can guide us toward a calmer state of mind, where we can become centered in the constructive elements of life and our divine possibilities.

The Meaning of the Symbols

The symbols used in this passage refer again to the metaphor of sheep and the shepherd's work. The primary need of sheep is for nourishment—grass and water—and the shepherd's duty is to lead the sheep to them.

While this need seems clear and obvious, most people today are uninformed about the habits of sheep and their special requirements. Of all the kinds of livestock that ranchers might have, sheep require an unusual amount of care and guidance.

A flock of sheep will tend to stay in one area until all of the vegetation is consumed, unless it is guided on to other areas. The sheep do not merely eat the grass, they can also devour the roots, thus depleting the pasture for some time. In other words, they will exhaust their resources and stay in an impoverished situation until the threat of starvation forces them to move on.

In a similar manner, sheep will tend to drink whatever water is available, regardless of its purity or freshness, unless someone guides them to better water. Once more, they readily tend to become stuck where they are and therefore need guidance to help them to better nourishment and fresh water.

Thus, the relationship between sheep and the shepherd is one of unexpected closeness. The shepherd must be unusually attentive and supportive to the sheep and supply guidance with great frequency. Unless this is done, the sheep will follow their instincts and inferior judgments, and their ability to thrive—or even survive—may be impaired.

Relating These Symbols to Our Human Condition

The symbology of guiding sheep to pasture and water is a clear message that we tend to limit ourselves to what is familiar and ordinary—even if it is impoverished, inadequate, or exhausted. Modern psychologists call this a tendency to stay in our "comfort zone." For various reasons—lack of imagination, lack of courage, or just plain stubbornness—we often fail to move on to better choices, situations, and opportunities. Some people are unwilling to change *even when they are fully aware of their distress*; they can recognize the conditions of their life are not supporting their health or emotional needs, but are too stubborn or too afraid to change. Because of this failure to change, they remain stuck in a relatively unproductive and unresourceful state far too long—perhaps indefinitely.

For instance, we might be stuck in a mood of pessimism or helplessness and just wallow in it, because we believe others are responsible for causing our difficulty—and therefore must fix it. We might continue to feel that we are being neglected or victimized, because we assume we can do nothing about it. Or we might be sick or worried and assume there is nothing more to do than suffer through this difficulty. All of these are situations where we feel unresourceful and undernourished in mind and heart—and perhaps even in body.

These are times when we need to *move to a different state of awareness and understanding*. We need to return to a more resourceful focus of mind—a more creative, energetic, optimistic, and courageous state of thought and feeling where we can rediscover our divine possibilities and learn how we can pursue them.

For us, therefore, the green pastures and quiet waters refer to the wellsprings of courage, wisdom, love, hope, and vitality in and about us. These are the qualities that nourish our humanity and restore our dignity. Our God calls us to enjoy a state of peace and strength where we can be refreshed, renewed, and healed.

The need for this kind of change is not reserved for just a few spiritually impoverished people. Most of us need to respond to this summons at frequent intervals. It is quite easy, for instance, to lose sight of our resources whenever we experience a major shock. We can just as easily become absorbed in an ongoing and prolonged, stressful condition. A habitually pessimistic and anxious person, for example, is often lost in fear and gloom and fails to recognize constructive possibilities. The chronically angry person is lost in the same fashion and fails to recognize the goodwill and acceptance that surrounds him.

This is why we need to have quick access to a "re-set button." In this case, calling on God to lead us to the human equivalent of green pastures and the quiet waters is extremely helpful.

The phrase "quiet waters" has one additional symbolic meaning for us. In the summer and fall months in many parts of the Middle East, the water supply in the pastures may be minimal or none. These are times when sheep rise early—before dawn in fact—to eat the grass while it is still wet with dew. This dew, consumed in sufficient quantities, can supply most of the water needed by the sheep. Therefore, "quiet waters" may refer to dew, which comes from the condensation of moisture in the air during the cooler hours of the night.

Dew symbolizes the gift from heaven of the living waters that nourish "the body not made by hand"—in other words, our character. In this sense, quiet waters refer to the spiritual love which comes from God and transcends all of our emotions. It does more than nourish—it heals and enriches us.

The ultimate message for us in this part of the psalm is this: God, as a wise and benevolent power, can guide us back from exhausted and impoverished states of thought and feeling and toward our inner strengths, talents, knowledge, serenity, faith, hope, and love. This shift of attention helps us to be more centered in our strengths and less focused on our distress or problems. As a result, we can find and explore better solutions to our problems or simply find an opportunity for rest and renewal.

The Spiritual Qualities and Insights Invoked

The three primary spiritual forces invoked by this stanza are:

1. *Guidance.* As we allow ourself to be open to the support of our divine possibilities, we are guided to higher levels of thought and feeling where insight, hope, and courage are more available to us.

2. *Calming.* As we move away from the struggles and strains of our outer experiences, we find a quiet oasis of serenity deep within us. This is where we can think more clearly and be more detached from the emotional stresses of our daily activities.

3. *Centering.* As we become more calm and shift our attention to our strengths, talents, knowledge, and

optimism, we move from outer anxiety and problems to being more focused in our healthy qualities and constructive possibilities. We also find that we have more faith in ourself and our support from divine intelligence. This lays the groundwork for the process of renewal as well as effective problem solving and confident activity.

Increasing Our Response to These Qualities

In order to respond fully to this stanza, we will need to cultivate attitudes of trust and openness to new and higher possibilities. We will also need to explore the higher dimensions of our life and character. To do this, we must be ready to seek out and entertain other parts of our character beyond our troubled and wounded habits and feelings. This is especially important if we have tended to become consumed by our sense of frustration and distress.

More specifically, we need to be ready to temporarily or permanently suspend our fears, anger, doubts, despair, or apathy to be open to other possibilities. We have to be ready to abandon our martyr complex, give up living in the past, or stop feeling so victimized and neglected. We must be ready to give up—at least for a time—our grudges, our habit of blaming and criticizing, our pursuit of vengeance, and our feelings of helplessness.

In short, we must make room in our awareness for more creative and constructive thinking and attitudes. This movement in awareness and attitude can be accomplished only as we do three things:

1. Remind ourself that we are never alone in our time of need or temptation, because we have the supportive and guiding help of our shepherding God.

2. Be willing to humble ourself to the degree that we can acknowledge that we are:

a) being overwhelmed by some aspects of life,

b) that we need help,

c) and are willing to accept it.

3. Recognize the fact that we have neglected to remember and tap into the parts of us that still know how to be calm, cheerful, optimistic, courageous, creative, and hopeful.

If we prepare ourself in this way, the powerful evocation of this stanza will summon us to this higher state of awareness—the figurative green pastures and quiet waters which nourish us in heart and mind.

Using This Stanza for Healing and Growth

There are three main ways this part of the 23rd Psalm can help us heal our attitudes:

1. To heal our fear of being overwhelmed. There are many situations which have the potential to overcome us. Unfortunately, our belief that we are inadequate often does more to undermine our success and well-being than whatever challenges us. This portion of the 23rd Psalm helps calm us, so we can return to our center, where we can gather our strengths and common sense to figure out what to do next.

2. To restore our dignity. If we insist on living our

life on the edge of anxiety, perceiving threats and hardship everywhere, we will quickly become uncertain about what to do. In short order, this uncertainty will expand to feeling unsure about our competence and self-worth. However, if we are convinced that our Creator can and will be guiding us and leading us to resources in and about us, we can face our challenges with calmness and dignity.

3. To help us find an inner serenity. Even when we know what to do and believe in our ability to do it, a feeling of stress may persist. An awareness of unresolved conflict and work yet to be done can leave us with a vague unrest. This is when we need to deepen our conviction that God is continuously on our side to help us, to add strength to our courage, confidence, and patience.

Summary

This portion focuses on our need for guidance and for centering in our strengths and resources for problem solving and healing. It calls us to an inner level of peace and faith in our competence and our divine possibilities. By being able to detach ourself from our outer challenges and difficulties, we can be open to the healthier and more powerful dimensions of character as well as our divine opportunities.

The key concepts this section emphasizes are:

1. God is our friend who loves us and keeps faith in *us* no matter how lost we feel or how hopeless our situation may seem to us.

2. God is our personal friend who can be trusted to guide us out of our difficulties and problems as we are willing to be open to change.

3. We can find the solutions and other resources we need to help ourself.

All of these realizations and efforts help us to cultivate greater cooperation and collaboration with our God.

Study Guide

1. How have I allowed pessimism, anger, fear, or apathy to sabotage my ability to respond to the advice and help of others or God?

2. Am I able to accept advice and counsel *only when* it is flattering and validates my beliefs?

3. Do I spend more time nursing my grievances than my divine opportunities?

4. Have I become so habituated to stress, anger, and gloom that I cannot imagine ever being free of them?

5. How would greater calmness and confidence change how I preceive my world and respond to its challenges?

chapter 7

HE RESTORES MY SOUL. HE GUIDES ME IN PATHS OF RIGHTEOUSNESS FOR HIS NAME S SAKE.

The Theme

The previous sections of this psalm have led us to a more conscious awareness of our divine opportunities and have helped to focus our attention on our strengths and other resources. This section deals with the need to reorient and revise our consciousness and generate a new motivation for being. We are helped to *reorient* to a more enlightened view of our self, life, and God—to see ourself as a spiritual being—the soul—and think as one. As this reorientation to a higher level of awareness and understanding occurs, it then is possible to *revise* and correct old ways of thought, belief, and behavior. The *motivation* for making these transformations also changes. As we become more conscious of ourself as a soul, we are motivated more by the will of our soul's purpose and plan. In other words, we respond to the spiritual will-to-be and impulse to grow towards wholeness, instead of our personality's wishes and wants.

The Meaning of the Symbols

"Restoring my soul" symbolically portrays the development of a new identity—of being called to return to a more enlightened state of awareness and understanding.

Being "guided in paths of righteousness" refers to mature and spiritual ways—paths—of thought, feeling, intention, and activity. In this instance, righteous means virtuous and aligned with higher intelligence and power—not self-righteous or holier-than-thou.

The phrase "for His name's sake" refers to our commitment to honor an inner, divine purpose and plan for being. The use of the word "name" suggests the concept of the secret essence or true nature of our self. In Biblical times, it was not unusual to accept a new name for one's self after a major transformation of character— as in the conversion of Saul to Paul. "For His name's sake" clearly suggests that the impulse for our new thinking, attitudes, and habits stems from a greater realization of the divine design for our new identity and orientation. In modern terms, this would be called a paradigm shift, which automatically leads to a new view of life and new beliefs.

Relating These Symbols To Our Human Condition

The concept of a soul is something that can be interpreted in a variety of ways. In psychological terms, the soul is the core of our character—the best within us. In other words, the soul is our major and enduring values, beliefs, knowledge, and habits. In spiritual terms, the word soul means something more. It refers to our innate and immortal spiritual self. In either case, "restores my soul" refers to the activation of an inner, basic, and more powerful level of knowledge and habits than we manifest in ordinary activities. The clear implication here is that we are complex beings who have many different levels of thought, feeling, and intention within us. The deeper or more inward we go, the closer we get to our most enlightened or spiritual essence.

The term "restores" also carries considerable significance in this context. We can only restore something that has had a previous history—returning to a more calm and creative state of mind. Beyond this concept, there is the clear hint that we exist first as a soul—a divine creation which is endowed with an original blessing of wisdom, love, courage, knowledge, talent, grace, vitality, and beauty. This is our permanent identity and true individuality, and one of the major purposes of living is to achieve some measure of this state of awareness and being and learn to express it in our own character and behavior.

Finally, we need to note the initial pronoun in this phrase, "*He* restores my soul." One of the primary purposes of prayer is to link our aspirations and devotions to our Creator's loving concern for us. With all the talk about the impersonal God, we tend to forget that our Creator is continually summoning us, through unconditioned love, to remember the glory we had with God before we became incarnate in a body and developed an earth-oriented personality. The fact is, our Creator is always calling us to "remember" who we are as an immortal soul with all of its attendant wisdom, love, power, and sense of oneness with God and all other souls.

If we return to the metaphor of sheep being guided by the good shepherd, we can see what the psalmist had in mind in using these simple words. First, the sheep are called to the green pastures and still waters to eat and drink. Then their "soul is restored" and they can be "led into the right paths." In the case of the sheep, the restoring of the soul means they have been nourished, refreshed, and renewed. They have been restored to their ideal condition as contented sheep.

The correspondence for us is remarkably similar. When we turn our attention to the source of our guidance, love, wisdom, strength, and peace, we also are nourished, refreshed, and renewed in mind, heart, and body. This leads us toward our ideal state—*the fulfillment of our spiritual design for wholeness.*

In our case, we nourish and refresh our mind by bringing it up to its peak performance and aligning it with its source of guidance and inspiration in God. We nourish and refresh our emotions by purifying them and renewing them with a full charge of love and joy. In a similar fashion, we nourish and refresh the body by bringing to it a full charge of vitality to renew its energy and function.

Through the activity of recharging our illumined mind, purified emotions, and healthy body with their ideal spiritual designs, we are truly restored to the soul. This is not just a case of adding more energy to the personality and body, however! The correct process actually *transforms* our beliefs, our outlook on life, and our sense of identity. In other words, the act of restoring our soul leads to a major *reorientation* about how we view ourself, our situation in life, and our relationship to God.

In this regard, a significant distinction must be made between *refreshment*—taking in new healing energies—versus *reorientation*—generating new beliefs, goals, and sense of identity. Refreshment occurs when we have rested and have increased the *quantity* or intensity of our faith, expectations, intentions, and beliefs. Reorientation occurs as we change the *quality* of our faith, expectations, intentions, and beliefs. This difference is quite significant.

Consider the state of tired, hungry, and thirsty sheep. Being lethargic, frustrated, and irritable, they are not going to be feeling or acting like normal sheep. They are not likely to be gentle, friendly, calm, or contented. They need food, water, and rest to refresh and restore them to being healthy, contented sheep.

In the same way, we can easily become exhausted, irritable, and frustrated from our efforts and burdens. Our faith, hope, and patience can wear thin. Our ability to think clearly and exercise our common sense can become fatigued. Our charitableness, tolerance, and self-control can be worn out from too much use. We need rest and the opportunity to restore our faith—and our mood—to more positive levels. We need a respite to clear out the mental cobwebs and restore our thinking and judgment to a more sensible state. We need rest and recreation to lift our spirits out of gloom and resentment and restore our usual capacity to accept and enjoy life. This is what it means to be refreshed and restored to our original state of thought, feeling, and expectation.

Once we are refreshed, the next step to take is reorientation. Recharging our energies is an important and useful first step, but "restoring the soul" calls us to a higher level of outlook, belief, and expectation. In this higher perspective, we can recognize more of our human and divine potential, see issues more clearly, and be more charitable in thought and feeling. In other words, we take on a new orientation or view of our self and our life.

There is a parallel here with the turning point in the parable of the prodigal son. Having wasted his inheritance and fallen on impoverished times, the prodigal son finally realizes his huge mistake and decides to "arise and return to his father." The words clearly equate "arising and returning" to a raising up of his understanding and a yearning to return to his father's benevolence as a new person, now humbled, patient, and wiser. This is an example of reorientation. It is not a minor change achieved by reshuffling attitudes; it is a complete redefinition of who we are and how we relate to our world.

Being rested and renewed, therefore, is substantially different from achieving a new orientation. Unfortunately, a true reorientation is so rare that many people are unfamiliar with the experience. As a result, many people desire only the pleasant, calm feeling of being rested, instead of seeking a new orientation to life.

The best way to dramatize the distinction between these two states is to notice how small the change is in irritable or pessimistic people between when they are rested versus when they are tired. Even when they are rested, the smallest event or comment can bring back snappish remarks and gloom. In the same way, the depressed person may feel slightly better when rested, but all of the latent unhappiness and impoverished beliefs are still there, ready to recreate an excess of despair at the slightest provocation. In other words, the rested, irritable person is still irritable, and the rested, depressed person is still gloomy at the level of their beliefs and sense of who they are.

A thorough reorientation of beliefs, self-image, and expectations is needed to begin effective healing. Rest— often no more than a temporary escape from burdens— and refreshment—getting our energy back—are like *first aid* rather than a definitive cure to our difficulties. Just as band-aids and aspirin are not enough for broken bones or tumors, so also encouragement and reassurance are usually not enough for broken confidence and the emotional "tumors" of resentment and anxiety. It is *change—* a reorientation in our basic beliefs about our self, strengths, and challenges—that begins the healing and growth needed for a permanent character transformation.

When we take time to withdraw from outer activities and thoughts, we can become more centered in our core strengths, talents, knowledge, and faith. We also can become more attuned to our spiritual self. This presents us with the opportunity to develop a new and more enlightened view of who we are and what our situation is. We will be able to look at old issues in new ways. We will be able to recognize constructive solutions that we had missed or dismissed before. We will be able to forgive what we had resented, tolerate what we had rejected, and accept what we had ignored. We will be able to find meaning and significance where we were apathetic. We will be able to appreciate what we took for granted. We will be able to find joy and fulfillment where we had found little.

These are the changes wrought by a healthy reorientation of our beliefs and attitudes, through the act of restoring our soul.

As our soul is restored and our outlook is uplifted on all issues, including ourself, the meaning of the second phrase, "He guides me in paths of righteousness," becomes clear. These are the paths of right thinking, attitudes, and habits. When we are centered in our innermost core of values, wisdom, and love of life, we can evaluate and plan in more enlightened and healthy ways. This is the first fruit of a genuine reorientation to our soul's wisdom and design for mature living.

Subsequently, we can begin to *act* on these new views and plans by converting them into new behavior and a more mature and enlightened lifestyle. This step, however, is not automatic. After all, we can be led to knowledge, by being given advice and encouragement, but we do not always recognize, accept, or use it. We can be loved and appreciated, but we can still feel inadequate. We can be entertained and cheered up, but still feel despondent inside. *New Paradigm.*

In order to use these resources, we need to cultivate new beliefs about our self, our past, our burdens, our strengths, our opportunities, our future, and our relationship to life and God. It is our responsibility to consume knowledge and *translate it into solutions*. We can easily consume loving thoughts and kindness, but it is our responsibility to translate them into tolerance, forgiveness, and cooperation. We can consume good cheer in happy times, but we need to translate this joy into optimism and enthusiasm for our daily activities. We can consume the encouragement and support of others, but we need to translate this support into endurance, perseverance, and new initiatives. We can be revitalized with strength and power, but we need to convert them into healing activities and health.

In this way, the new paths of awareness lead us to explore and discover our divine possibilities and then to demonstrate them as part of a more healthy and mature character and self-expression.

The statement that God guides us in the paths of righteousness concludes with these cryptic words: "for his name's sake." This short phrase explains why we are going to make all of these changes. A simple desire for better times is not the most noble or enduring motive to impel us toward health and wholeness. We need a stronger, more altruistic motive. We often hear parents speak of doing something "for the sake of" their children. This attitude of sacrifice captures the essence of a noble motivation: they are not doing something for personal benefit so much as because it is the "right thing." So also, we are called to change our beliefs and behavior "for the sake" of our Creator's Plan and love for us. This means we seek to honor His will—"His name"—and do something because our Creator wills it for us—"for His sake."

The Spiritual Qualities and Insights Invoked

This part of the psalm tells us several things and presents to us many wonderful opportunities. These are:

1. That we have a core or inner self—the soul—which is the site of all of our human and divine potential for strength, wisdom, talents, love, joy, patience, and all other fruits and gifts of spirit.

2. This soul is the true home of our individuality. We are called to accept, understand, and work with it as a companion in all worthwhile endeavors.

3. This inner core of strength and healing love is available to us as a powerful resource for healing, renewal, and enrichment.

Increasing Our Response to These Qualities

There are a number of lessons in living this section of the psalm encourages us to master:

1. **Cultivating detachment.** Without ignoring or denying our duties and problems, we need to take time to detach periodically from our concern about outer events. As we do this, we need to deepen our realization that we are always more than just our body, feelings, and thoughts. More importantly, we are certainly more than our hurts, losses, illness, or fears. We are also more than our unhappy memories or our anxiety about our future. Our darkest moments and worst suffering may be poignant, but they never can describe more than one moment's experience for us. Who we are is something far greater and more powerful. If we can cultivate detachment in this manner, we will be prepared to engage in the reorientation to the life of the soul.

2. **Identifying with our strengths and abilities.** Detachment is an activity which prepares us to identify with our inner intelligence and courage—not just admire it. Even in the midst of illness, we need to think of ourself as a potentially healthy person who is temporarily experiencing some symptoms. Just so, even when we are disappointed by a failure, we need to think of ourself as a resourceful person who has the capacity to recoup our losses and repair our mistakes. Detachment does not mean that we ignore problems; it means we are able to work with our strengths as constructively as possible.

How do we gain this kind of detachment? By learning to identify with our problem solving abilities more than our problems, with our capacity for tolerance and forgiveness more than our resentments, and with our healing abilities more than our illnesses. In other words, we need to turn our full attention to the source of our strength to endure and our wisdom to solve problems. At the same time, detachment helps us rediscover the love to tolerate and forgive, the joy to sustain hope and enthusiasm, and the vitality to heal and sustain ourself. By being able to identify with our human strengths and resources in this way, we also prepare ourself to identify with our soul's design and plan.

3. **Leading an examined life.** By frequently reviewing our experiences and choices, we cultivate the attentiveness and habits essential to growth. Good advice, object lessons, and unexpected results are more likely to be recognized. The belief that we always have more to learn keeps us keenly interested in new ideas and approaches to old problems and opportunities. These attitudes prepare us to participate in the complete redefinition that comes as we are reoriented to our soul's consciousness.

4. **Adaptability.** As we cultivate a wholesome flexibility, we are better able to engage in healthy change and the growth of our beliefs and understanding. It is one thing to admire new ideas and crave good feelings, but these are fleeting experiences that have no enduring value—unless we can integrate them into our beliefs

and habits of behavior. Genuine change and growth require a restructuring of our mainstream beliefs, intentions, and habits into healthier patterns. This work unfolds as we learn to draw our old beliefs of gloom into newly rediscovered optimism, confidence, and enthusiasm—or draw old beliefs about limitation into new ones about our competence and freedom. In these and similar ways, we prepare ourself to be guided in "paths of righteousness"—that is, healthy patterns of thought and behavior.

Using This Stanza for Healing and Growth

This stanza promotes healing and growth in several important ways:

1. **To heal our fear of being incompetent.** As we learn to believe in, trust, and accept the fact of our spiritual core, we can begin to use it as a valuable resource for all of our important needs. Later, as we incorporate it as our true identity and the very essence of our character, we can establish a more enduring state of confidence based on the conviction that our Creator has designed us to be whole, noble, healthy, and fulfilled.

2. **To heal our fear of losing control.** Our Creator is continually *summoning us* to find rest in our divine nature and to know and experience the serenity, love, insight, and strength that can be found there. As we experience this sense of poise and dignity, we are also going to be more in command of ourself and our situation.

3. **To heal our sense of indecision and confusion.** As we open ourself to the support and guidance of our Creator, we begin to believe and trust that there is a way out for us. In other words, *God has a Plan for us.* There is a divine destiny for us, and there are rules to guide us on our way. We may feel confused, but there is an answer for us.

4. **To heal our fear of failure.** As we allow ourself to be led into the right paths of thought, attitude, and intention, we become more convinced that our Creator supports all of our worthwhile efforts to learn, grow, heal, and improve. We are never alone in our sincere efforts to make sense of our experiences and choose the right way to think and feel about life or how to act.

Summary

This portion of the psalm tells us that God is continually calling us to an inner level of thought and feeling where we can rediscover our innate and divine design for wholeness. Being refreshed by the right mental and emotional food and water is just a beginning. The next step is contact with God's Plan and power for us. When we are inwardly nourished and content, we can find our human center of understanding, calmness, and positive expectation. From this human center, we can reach higher to our soul and its guiding wisdom, uplifting love and joy, and empowering strength. As we embrace these qualities, we are led to new paths of perspective and attitude about who we are and where we are headed.

Study Guide

1. Am I still demanding that others make me happy and well, or do I recognize my responsibility to fully participate in this effort? What have I done to demonstrate this personal responsibility?

2. To what degree am I aware that the pattern of my beliefs (rather than outer events and other people) are responsible for recreating much of my resentment, sadness, apathy, and anxiety?

3. Do I realize that the new "paths of righteousness" for me mean I may need to change my sense of who I am and my expectations? Do I understand this must be done *before* I become more happy, healthy, and fulfilled?

4. How often and how well do I recognize my soul as a resource for healing and growth? Do I expect it to do all the work, or do I expect to *work with it* in translating its guidance into new understanding and behavior?

chapter 8

EVEN THOUGH I WALK THROUGH THE VALLEY OF THE SHADOW OF DEATH, I WILL FEAR NO EVIL, FOR YOU ARE WITH ME; YOUR ROD AND YOUR STAFF, THEY COMFORT ME.

The Theme

Up to this point, the 23rd Psalm has helped us become detached from our distress and more aligned with our divine resources and origins. The psalm now concentrates fully on invoking divine powers to help us. These words call on divine power to protect us in times of distress. More specifically, this part of the psalm summons divine energies to dispel our fears and doubts and to build our calmness, confidence, and courage. In other words, the purpose of this part is to purge negative qualities from our character and lift us up to a higher level of thought and feeling.

The Meaning of the Symbols

Some of the most difficult work of the shepherd came

at the time of moving the flock to higher pastures in the spring—and when returning them to their home in the fall. These journeys were always fraught with danger.

The *"valley of the shadow of death"* refers to the valleys leading to these higher pastures. The valleys were chosen because they were more likely to be full of plants to eat and sufficient water. However, death also lurked within them, in the form of predatory animals who could hide in nearby places. Death quite literally stalked the sheep throughout these journeys.

The shepherd needed something to help him drive off these predators. This was his "rod." Usually, this was a wooden club, sometimes with nails protruding from it. *The rod came to symbolize the shepherd's power to dispel destructive forces.*

The shepherd's "staff" served quite a different purpose. It was not to help the shepherd walk the rough ground. Rather, it was used to lift the sheep (especially the lambs) out of places where they had fallen into holes or crevices. Also, at the time of birth, new lambs were lifted by the staff to be next to the mother, because touching them by hand might leave a human scent that could cause the mother to reject their own offspring. *The staff came to symbolize the shepherd's power to preserve the life of the sheep.*

Relating These Symbols to Our Human Condition

Once more, the poetic example of a shepherd leading his flock reveals the nature of our relationship to our Creator. "The valley of the shadow of death" refers to any potential for danger. Parallel to the journey of the sheep, we often choose or are compelled to move from one stage of our life to another. This more figurative journey can bring us into confrontation with unexpected risks and danger. This is the shadow or threat which accompanies us throughout our life.

In common usage, the "valley experience" refers to times of danger, confusion, loss, despair, and neglect. These are the darkest hours, when we are weakest and most uncertain. They are, therefore, times when we most need extra guidance and protection.

The use of the term "evil" in this context describes anything that would threaten our survival or highest good. For the sheep, this is not a diabolical force so much as it is the potential of attack by predators, sudden storms, early blizzards, the lack of water in the fall, poisonous plants the sheep might eat, and other factors. For us, evil is not just something that makes us uncomfortable or unhappy. After all, confronting the consequences of what we have done or left undone might be very unpleasant for us, but it would also be an act of honoring our highest good. In this sense, then, "evil" would be anything—within or without us—that might interfere with reaching or expressing our highest good.

We need to remember that being devoted and willing to follow our Creator's guidance does not mean a life free of pain and suffering; it means that we will be protected and sustained in our times of difficulty. We sometimes forget that God may choose to calm us instead of calming the storm around us. This is still divine protection. If we keep the faith in ourself and the Intelligence that guides us, we grow stronger in our ability to endure in hard times.

In the language of the psalm, the shepherd was always with his sheep, especially in the times of difficulty. He would scout the trail ahead to find the best passage, water to drink, and places to be avoided—for example, where poisonous plants might kill the sheep. He would also be on the lookout for predators. And, always, he would be attentive to those sheep that became separated from the flock so he could lead them back. So also, our Creator is always with us. We may not recognize or believe in this. In fact, we may feel alone or abandoned, but this is an illusion born of our despair and fear. It is a false assumption.

The power of this metaphor to comfort us lies in the fact that our Creator is always with us to guide, protect, and preserve our life and well-being. We may feel lost, but our Creator does not lose us. We may be in real danger, but our Creator will protect us. We may not know that some life choices we might make are figuratively poisonous, but our Creator does. Those who trust in divine guidance will receive it.

The Spiritual Qualities and Insights Invoked

The psalm clearly states that *God is with us*. This means our Creator is accessible—not remote. God cares deeply about us and our well-being—just like the shepherd cares about his flock. If we are lost, He will go after us. If we are stuck, He will help lift us out of the hole that has trapped us. If we are confused, He will guide us. If we are thirsty and hungry, He will lead us to nourishment and refreshment. If we are in danger, He will protect us. God is with us as our friend, guide, protector, and healer. We have a rich endowment of undiscovered blessings and strength deep within us. These are our treasures of spirit.

Some of the major gifts in this endowment are:

1. Comfort. We are not alone or defenseless. God is with us at our point of need.

2. Confidence. We have a divine champion in times of great danger and risk. We have God on our side to help us in all worthwhile endeavors.

3. Hope. Divine power and divine order are guiding, supporting, and protecting us. Divine support is always available to help us.

4. Endurance. Our Creator is a powerful, indwelling resource for our protection and healing—a core of strength greater than any threat, illness, or danger we may encounter. We will endure.

Increasing Our Response to These Qualities

We must be aware that while opportunities and help may be offered to us, we have the power (unlike the sheep), to ignore or refuse what is offered. We can refuse to accept guidance and go off on paths that lead to nowhere. We can refuse warnings that the continued pursuit of our fears and temptations might lead to great danger. We can even refuse the blessings that are offered to us if we decide we are unworthy and undeserving.

In fact, the forces of fear, anger, and despair can blind us so totally that we will no longer respond to the support of either our friends or our Creator. We therefore need to keep open the channels that lead to divine support.

For this reason, we must be vigilant, making sure that our tendency to doubt and despair does not block our channels to God. We must exercise instead our faith and trust in divine support. We must be ready to accept and cooperate with divine guidance—especially when it is not flattering and when it does not conform to our preferences. Most of all, we must seek to meet God at our point of faith and hope, not our grief and guilt.

Beyond cultivating a wholesome faith, we must be ready to cooperate with and contribute to our well-being—to act on divine guidance and direction. We need to be able to embrace good suggestions. We must also be ready to discipline any tendency to take the path of least resistance and return to old habits.

Above all, we need to keep the faith that we are God's child and as such have a divine inheritance. This inheritance includes the power to protect and preserve the goodness in our life. It is this divine legacy that makes us and our life worthwhile, even in times of trouble and tragedy.

Using This Stanza for Growth and Healing

This part of the psalm is exceptionally powerful for those in need of comfort and reassurance in times of confusion and loss. We may feel that our life is broken or that we are broken in vital areas; we are overwhelmed with the reality before us. These are the moments when we need to take our wounds and hurts to our divine Creator for repair, renewal, and healing.

Just as the sheep have learned to trust their shepherd, we too must learn to trust and abide in the support and love of our Creator. This part of the 23rd Psalm summons the power of God to protect, guide, and preserve the quality of our life and our ability to endure in difficult times. The most helpful way to use the qualities invoked in this part is for these needs:

1. To heal despair and aloneness.
2. To neutralize fear and anger.
3. To resolve confusion and indecision.
4. To purge guilt and feelings of unworthiness.
5. To help in overcoming temptation.

Summary

The importance of the right state of mind, attitude, and expectation for effectiveness in prayer and invocation is far too often neglected. As long as we are obsessed with our needs, wants, and suffering, we tend to stay earthbound—we concentrate on our problems, illnesses, distresses, or fears. Our thoughts of prayer and supplication can be drowned out by our attention to despair and distress. We may earnestly need help, yet doubt our ability to receive it, so long as we are mired in painful feelings and sensations. If we can become detached and more reoriented to our source of help in spirit, then we will be able to open a more effective channel to divine powers.

We therefore need to seek divine support *to dispel fear as a problem in itself,* in addition to resolving the situation that triggered this fear. Many people forget that God is much more than a cuddly presence that sends us warm, fuzzy feelings of sweetness. God is a power that dispels and neutralizes discordant forces which truly can harm us. We can rely on prayer to summon this assistance to empower us to endure, survive, and thrive even as difficult situations continue in our life.

Study guide

1. How do we know that something in our life is truly harmful to our well-being? What are our criteria for deciding what is helpful and what is not? Is everything that makes us feel bad truly a bad thing for us?

2. How has God's protection manifested for us? How might it manifest in our future? Will it come from outside of us? Or will it be as something that occurs within us?

3. Recall a time when God calmed you instead of the storm—the ongoing conflict around you. What was it like? How did this change you? How has this changed your relationship to God?

chapter 9

YOU PREPARE A TABLE BEFORE ME IN THE PRESENCE OF MY ENEMIES. YOU ANOINT MY HEAD WITH OIL; MY CUP OVERFLOWS.

The Theme

We now come to a part of the 23rd Psalm which stresses the power of God to enrich—not merely heal—our character. The previous parts of this psalm have helped us become calm and centered in the best within us, drawn us into the presence of our spiritual Creator, and dispelled our fears. Now we are ready to receive and respond to the blessings our Creator has prepared for us.

The phrases of this part of the psalm invoke qualities and insights which can enlighten and enrich our character. They bring us into a higher realm of consciousness—the heavenly state of awareness and knowing—where we can tap the spiritual wellsprings of our ability to experience and express our inner wisdom, love, joy, courage, and talents.

The Meaning of the Symbols

Remembering that this psalm draws on the metaphor of a good shepherd with his flock of sheep, we can examine what is meant by "table," "anointing," and "our cup overflowing."

Other translations substitute the words "banquet" or "feast" for "table." These terms refer to the great abundance of God's blessings for us. The clear implication is that our God is a very generous God—not stingy and miserly. We are to be treated to a bountiful supply—more than we can use. This spiritual abundance must be interpreted in terms of an abundance of *all* good things—not just material blessings, but an abundance of wisdom, peace, goodwill, joy, serenity, confidence, self-respect, contentment, and hope.

The term "table" has a special meaning in the context of this metaphor. The pasture land in the Palestinian area, as well as many parts of the world, contain plants which can be harmful or poisonous to sheep. The shepherd might well go about the pasture to remove such plants and otherwise prepare the pasture—the "table" or place where the sheep eat. In much the same way, our Creator goes before us to prepare our way—to make it safe and provide opportunity to nourish our dignity and health of mind and body.

This preparation of the table is done "in the presence of my enemies." The enemies of the sheep are its predators (wolves, insects, snakes) as well as poisonous plants. Other enemies would be less tangible, such as drought, excessive heat, and thirst. Herding sheep to pasture automatically would attract those predators that view sheep as their next meal. Hence, the shepherd was always vigilant and worked with a mindfulness of the constant risk to him and his flock. Once more, the divine power to preserve and protect life is being emphasized in this poetic reference.

"Anoint my head with oil" is a reference to the common practice of the shepherd to put medicated oil or salve on the heads of sheep. Sheep, like most outdoor animals, suffer terribly from insect bites and abrasions to their face as they graze. These bites and cuts can attract more insects and become infected. The oil is the medication that soothes these problems.

Therefore, being "anointed" on the head refers to our Creator's capacity to comfort us at our point of need, whatever that might be. It reaffirms God's infinite capacity to provide for our needs and bless us.

"My cup overflows" is a reference to the abundance of help and blessings available in divine sources. The shepherd was willing to go the extra mile to assist his sheep—to give as much as was needed and then some. So also, our Creator is ready and able to give as much as we are willing to receive—and a lot more.

Relating These Symbols to Our Human Condition

The first part of this stanza stresses the nature of our Creator. Not only is the shepherd a source of protection and benevolence, but he also is *generous*. Our Creator is a gracious host who freely gives us what we need—and more. We are being offered a banquet of all good things.

Just as importantly, this part of the psalm spells out more details about the nature of our relationship to our Creator. Our Creator is not miserly or indifferent to our need. In fact, God is exactly the opposite: caring, devoted to what is best for us, deeply involved in our survival, protection, thriving, and daily nourishment.

There are also indications that the spiritual life is blessed with an abundance of all good things. We are not just given what we need—we are given what we need to the point where it "overflows" us. This confirms the abundance of support, protection, and nurturing love that God stands ready to provide.

In essence, these phrases are telling us that God has a plan for us. Our life is not designed to be chaotic; nor are we ever at the complete mercy of external events. There is a destiny for us, an inner, spiritual design for living that our Creator has set for us.

In addition to revealing more about our Creator and our relationship to God, this part of the psalm reveals something of how our Creator supports us. The specific words are that "a table or banquet is prepared for us." The shepherd *leads* the flock to the green pastures and still waters. But the shepherd does not eat or drink for them. The sheep must recognize their bounty and then do their own drinking and nourish themselves.

In other words, the guidance, protection, and aid that

our Creator provides may be direct and tangible—but more often than not, His guidance will be presented as suggestions, hints, or object lessons. His support and abundance are presented as potential to be developed—by us.

As the "table" for the sheep is their pasture, the table for us is the whole of our life. The "table" might be a damaged relationship that needs some healing. It could be our career that is in danger of going under. It might be our health of mind or body. It could also be the confused and faltering relationship we have with our conscience and our spiritual design. These are some of the fields of thought and endeavor that our Creator goes to prepare for us.

Just as sheep have their enemies, so we all have ours. The sheep's enemies are mostly tangible, in the form of dangerous predators or harsh weather, or as the conspicuous lack of food and water.

Our enemies are usually more subtle. Unlike the sheep, our enemies are not viewing us as their next meal, but they may be ready to destroy our faith, joy, health, and success in key areas of our life. They may be eager to undermine our confidence, interfere with our career, sabotage our relationships, steal our creative ideas, or cause us to neglect our legitimate needs.

While some of our enemies are very well known to us, many of our enemies will be invisible as well as subtle. In fact, some of life's most persistent and destructive enemies lurk within us, in the form of our persistent doubts, fears, resentments, guilt, and despair. Because of their indwelling and continual influence, they can be more of a problem for us than external enemies.

It is exactly in these areas of danger and conflict that divine support and protection can be most available and useful. Our prayers and meditations can attune us to the divine blessings God has already placed within us. But it is up to us to activate our latent courage to cope with our conscious fears and doubts. It is up to us to mobilize our potential for love to forgive those things that still overwhelm us with resentment. It is up to us to stimulate our capacity for problem solving and thinking to tap the guidance we need to find the way out of our current difficulties. In these ways, we learn to summon divine support to cope with our internal enemies of negativity, limiting beliefs, destructive urges, and apathy.

As the heads of the sheep are "anointed" with oil to provide comfort for their cuts and insect bites, so also, we are anointed with spiritual qualities and blessings that soothe us from whatever has "bitten" our confidence or "cut" into our health and success. Our anointing may be the divine blessing of strength to endure, the vitality to renew ourself, a strengthening of our faith in the value of our goals and activities, or a sense of fulfillment in our ongoing struggle.

These quiet miracles can be experienced each day by those who seek to attune to their divine possibilities and are willing to participate in activating them. The comfort and reassurance we need in confusing and difficult times truly are the proof that "our cup overflows" in time of need.

The Spiritual Qualities and Insights Invoked

There are several new realizations that emerge in our understanding as we reflect on this passage. They include:

1. Security. God goes with us and before us to prepare our day and our work. Divine guidance and protection are available. The life of spirit is an indwelling, constantly available source of power, love, wisdom, and joy to help us at all times.

2. Abundance. God dwells in us as an abundance of all good qualities and strengths we need to help us endure and thrive. Opportunity and helpful resources are to be found in both obvious and hidden areas of our immediate situation.

3. There is a divine design for our destiny. There is an underlying divine order and plan for us to be successful and fulfilled. The way out of any discordance and chaos in our situation is to embrace the power and guidance of this divine order and plan.

4. We are already blessed in many important ways. We have already been given insights, virtues, and opportunities to improve the quality of our life. As we recognize, appreciate, and use them more fully, our Creator will renew and enrich these blessings.

Increasing Our Response To These Qualities

It is vital to appreciate that God's blessings for us will fall on infertile soil unless we are ready to receive and use them. Our Creator can offer the opportunities and benefits we need, but we must recognize and cultivate them. God cannot guarantee that we will register them, because we may ignore them or turn away from them. Many a person has lamented the impoverishment of love and security in their life simply because they could not accept what was offered. Sometimes this is because they thought they were unworthy. Sometimes it was because they could not recognize the offer, or did not trust the situation or person that would lead to the blessing. At other times, people fail to accept their abundance because they are drowning in pessimism, fear, or resentment; these dark moods blind them to the presence of divine opportunities.

Still others fail to receive their blessings because they assume the blessings will arrive as a simple gift—and they will need to do nothing to activate them.

Many people choose to ignore the fact that we need to prepare ourself with knowledge and skill in order to receive inspiration and guidance. The great masterpieces of art, music, and literature come only to those who have mastered the skills of their profession. Likewise, great scientific advances come only to those who have the training and skills to add to the growing tip of their field. Clearly, the size of our cup—our capacity to receive inspiration—depends on the amount of knowledge and skill we can bring to the wisdom God is ready to give us.

It should be obvious, therefore, that our readiness to involve ourself in developing our divine possibilities is essential to leading a fulfilling life graced with an abundance of all good things. It is our preparation to receive God's blessings which determines the size of our "cup."

In the poetic language of the psalm, our cup is our ability to appreciate our worthiness as a child of God and to expect great things. As a child of God, we have a divine inheritance of many wonderful things. If we doubt this, we diminish the size of our cup—our ability to receive. If we are cynical, apathetic, or resentful about hardships, we reduce the size of our capacity to receive confidence, courage, and hope. If we are full of guilt, despair, and shame, we likewise decrease our ability to receive the very blessings we seek.

It is imperative that we meet every important condition in our life with faith, hope, and devotion to the best in us and our situation. For this reason, we will connect to our divine blessings better on a wavelength of positive expectation—a willingness to collaborate with our divine design for wholeness. Where we are cut by the criticism and condemnation of others, our Creator can offer us comfort. Where we are bitten by the shame of our own failure, divine blessings can come to lift us out of our despair. Our spiritual life becomes far more abundant in this way.

Using This Stanza for Healing and Growth

As we respect our innate spiritual qualities and design, we come to appreciate the many daily opportunities to turn toward spirit for help. This part of the 23rd Psalm is especially good to help us in these areas of need:

1. The feeling of emptiness or impoverishment. We assume that we are almost psychologically bankrupt and incapable of doing more—as if the wellsprings of our stamina, faith, and abilities are empty.

2. The sense of abandonment and rejection. We believe that we are standing alone in an apathetic or hostile world.

3. The feeling that we are under attack. We become convinced that we are succumbing to the efforts of others who are sabotaging our well-being.

4. Strong doubts and feelings of inferiority. Our own fears and insecurities become our worst enemies.

Summary

Our God is constantly on duty to protect us. This protection is provided in various ways. One way is to prepare our path by removing some obstacles and dangers to our well being. God also provides us with sufficient courage, knowledge, and faith to endure times of difficulty. Our Creator likewise provides rich opportunities for us to develop new skills, cultivate greater confidence, and build the success we seek.

When our difficulties come from within us (in the form of destructive attitudes, urges, and habits), God can be exceptionally helpful. The dark side of our own nature may often sabotage our health and happiness, but divine qualities and possibilities also dwell deep within us. They are available to help us in our time of personal conflict.

Most of all, this part of the psalm reminds us that we are meant to live life fully—with an abundance of all good things. We are meant to express hope, joy, courage, wisdom, and the power to bring these qualities into manifestation in who we are and what we do.

Study Guide

1. What opportunities are available for you today to heal and grow? What are you going to do about them?

2. What opportunities have you rejected in the past? Why did you do this? What does this reveal about your beliefs?

3. Who are your real enemies? How often does your indifference, distrust, or pessimism undermine your success and happiness? What are you going to do about this?

4. What is the "size of your cup?" How optimistic are your expectations of success? How much faith do you have in your worth and the worthiness of your goals? Are you are as ready to receive as God is ready to provide for you?

chapter 10

SURELY GOODNESS AND LOVE WILL FOLLOW ME ALL THE DAYS OF MY LIFE, AND I WILL DWELL IN THE HOUSE OF THE LORD FOREVER.

The Theme

Up to this point, this psalm has told us that God will *lead* us to quiet waters, *restore* our soul, *guide* us in right paths, *comfort* us, *prepare* a table for us, and *anoint* our head. Now we are informed that goodness and love will *follow* us and that we will *dwell* in the house of the Lord. Clearly, the fact of God's presence in our life is being emphasized in all possible ways.

In this part of the 23rd Psalm, we are being reminded that our Creator is behind us, supporting us all the way. That is, God's benevolent care and intent are active forces in our lives all the time, regardless of our poor judgment, failure, or other mistakes. In strongest possible terms, we are being told that we live with God; that is, we live and move and have our being in the divine presence. As a fish swims in water, so also, we are immersed in the love and goodness of spirit. We thrive because of this fact.

The Meaning of the Symbols

The "house of the Lord" mentioned in the psalm is not a physical structure or temple. Nor is it membership in a religious group. These things can easily come and go in our life, and neither of them can guarantee either love or goodness for us.

The house of the Lord is our spiritual body—the soul—which is the dwelling place of our permanent or spiritual essence. It is the body and form of our higher self or supraconscious self. It lives or dwells on the sublime plane of divine archetypal forces. Therefore, it always rests in an environment of spiritual light, love, and wholeness.

Relating These Symbols to our Human Condition

The "goodness and love" mentioned in this passage is of the spiritual type—not the common social variety of politeness and niceness. Other translations of the psalms capture this more substantive meaning when they use the terms "charity" and "mercy." In the context of this part of the 23rd Psalm, we are told that goodness and love will follow us. In other words, good purpose and plans will guide our destiny, goodwill will support our struggles, charitable love will enfold us in our mistakes and transgressions, and merciful love will redeem us in our darkest hours of shame and remorse.

These promises foretell the example of the merciful father in the story of the prodigal son. In this parable, the father, symbolizing the benevolence and generosity of our Creator-Parent, allows the son to waste his birthright and then mercifully accepts him on his return as one who is now a wiser, contrite, and humbled person. In this way, the parable highlights the quality of goodness and love in which we dwell forever.

When we are told that we will dwell in the house of the Lord forever, we are being reminded that our spiritual essence—the soul—is always available to us; it is not something remote or out of touch for us. Nor are we just an occasional visitor in the household of spirit. We are not like the slave that comes timidly into the master's presence. We are part of the household of God, part of the family of all of God's children. We are automatically accepted and endowed with the blessing of a spiritual birthright of wisdom, compassion, joy, and all the other fruits of the spirit. Therefore, we can say that we "dwell in the house of the Lord forever. "

Of course, many people believe this principle *without comprehending it.* Even fewer demonstrate it in their lives. This is because a full realization of our dwelling in the house of the Lord depends on cultivating a spiritualized state of thought, feeling, and purpose.

As our consciousness expands to include an awareness of our innermost essence, we become attuned to our spiritual wellsprings of wisdom, joy, love, and courage. As we incorporate these insights and qualities into our beliefs and habits, we grow in consciousness. We reform our sense of identity, values, attitudes, and the way we interact with our challenges and opportunities. As we begin to act as our Creator would have us behave, we align ourself with our divine design more fully and embrace all of our divine possibilities.

Another term for this level of collaboration is "heaven." In other words, the house of the Lord is the same as the Kingdom of Heaven within us.

As we fully comprehend the significance of this part of the psalm, we come to believe and understand that God is with us all the time—not just after death, but here, now, and always. God's loving care and support is with us in times of trial and triumph. God's love is with us in our moments of sadness and joy, in sickness and health, and in our tragedies as well as our successes.

We are also reminded that the dominant characteristic of our Creator is benevolence—a charitable, merciful love. God does not restrict divine blessings or punish us. We experience impoverishment and difficulty because we neglect to choose and act as our Creator has designed us to do. And so, when we stray from the ideal path or method, God's goodness and love is there to help us recover, reform our ways, and redeem ourself.

The Spiritual Qualities and Insights Invoked

The final part of the 23rd Psalm is extraordinarily rich in meaning for us. The most significant qualities and insights invoked are:

1. **The immanence of God**—the insight that God's love and goodness will be with us whatever happens to us. We may feel—as a personality—abandoned and alone, but our Creator's love and support is always with us. We are divinely designed and endowed to be healthy, whole, and productive.

2. **God's unlimited faith in us.** We may make huge mistakes and disgrace ourself, but divine mercy and good-will are always available to help heal, renew, and reform us.

3. **Optimism.** We can be more optimistic because we have a great benevolent power at work in our life, guiding our choices, protecting our activities, support-ing our struggles, and rewarding our good efforts.

Increasing Our Response to These Qualities

It is not enough to *believe* in good ideas. We need to *be good and do good*. We must actively seek to com-prehend and demonstrate wisdom in our understand-ing and behavior.

Therefore, if we seek to increase our attunement to God's love and goodness for us, we need to practice dedi-cation to the highest good within us. We need to aspire to all of our divine possibilities. We need to dwell fre-quently on the fact that, in some mysterious way, our origin and destiny are both divine. We need to take com-fort in the fact that we have been created out of God's perfect wisdom and love. We need to feel encouraged that there is a divine plan for our life and lifestyle—a plan that inspires us to move toward our destined wholeness.

At all times, especially in our darkest hours, we need to remember these things and ponder on their significance to us. If we do, we can arrest our natural tendency to surrender to the voice of materialism and the messages of our senses. When we are tempted to feel alienated and abandoned, we can be reminded that a power greater than any person or group loves and supports us. When we are tempted to believe that there is nothing else we can do, we can ask for divine assistance to do what we cannot do alone. When we are tempted to believe our life has no purpose or meaning, we can draw on divine guidance to help us find meaning in our struggle.

When we stop thinking of God as an external power to be worshipped from afar, and come to regard God as an indwelling resource which can heal and comfort us, we can change our lives. With this practical approach to our divine possibilities, we can accelerate the movement of new spiritual direction, qualities, and strength into our minds and hearts.

Using This Stanza for Healing and Growth

The qualities and insights invoked in this part of the psalm are so general in scope that they have global benefits. They can be used for almost any kind of psychological or physical need, or for problems in our domestic life and careers. However, the forces invoked in this part are exceptionally useful in meeting the following needs:

1. **Brokenness.** Sometimes we come to the realization that something about our life is not working, because we lack a major skill or quality, and we may never find it. It appears that we are irreparably broken, and no external help can assist us. This is when we need to return to our spiritual essence for the power to heal us at a deep level.

2. **The absence of meaning and relevance to our struggle.** When our ongoing struggle seems useless and hopeless, we are headed toward burn out. We need to visit spiritual headquarters for a fresh vision and understanding about the relevance of what we are doing and our spiritual purpose in life.

3. **Aloneness.** Sometimes our special problems make us feel very isolated—as if we are some kind of a leper. We may receive sympathy, but without real empathy or understanding of our experience. Help may be offered to us, but it is not what we need to sustain us and fill the emptiness in us. We need to strengthen our personal relationship with our Creator and the goodness and love that comes from this enduring source.

4. **Guilt and shame.** There are occasions when we feel we have committed an unpardonable sin, have made a monstrous mistake, or have lost an irreplaceable opportunity. Even worse, we may be convinced that it is all our fault. In this lowly condition, we need more than a temporary repair; we need forgiveness, renewal, and

a resurrection of our faith in ourself, our life, and our Creator.

Summary

God is a continuous presence of divine guidance, benevolence, protection, and encouragement. Moreover, our relation to God is profoundly intimate—we dwell in the house of the Lord forever. This means that there has never been a time when the presence of divine influences was not available to us—neither before birth, nor during physical life, nor after our physical death.

Our spiritual essence is our true and permanent identity. We are never without our lines of support from a sublime and benevolent source. We may forget about our spiritual support, but it is still there, like the ground under our feet. We may ignore it, but it is there like water in our mouth. We may deny it, but it is still there like air in our lungs.

As we appreciate the fact of our Creator's benevolent nature and fully accept it into our life, we come to live with dignity and grace—we live in the consciousness of the Lord. For this reason, goodness and love follow us all our days.

Study Guide

1. How have we benefited from charitable love and mercy in our life? Where can we point to what seems to have been a divine intervention in coping with some major loss or mistake?

2. Have we recognized the times when divine benevolence, support, and guidance has arrived *through* some human agency?

3. Since divine guidance and support can also come from deep within us, how do we recognize them? Is the subtlety of object lessons lost on us? Can we recognize the message embedded in a pattern of failure or adversity? Or in a pattern of success?

4. Beyond simple belief, what are we prepared to do to summon and absorb the power and design of divine guidance?

5. How often are we ready to let divine intelligence define what is best for us? How often are we prepared to accept this definition when it differs from our personal preference?

chapter 11

USING THE 23rd PSALM
FOR HEALING AND GROWTH

Working with prayer and invocation is like speaking. Words can be expressed in a meaningful way that conveys information clearly and lyrically. Or we can mumble and hesitate and choose words in a such a clumsy manner that our speech is confused and conceals more than it communicates.

It is possible to mentally recite the ancient words of the 23rd Psalm with no more understanding or reverence than we would give to last week's shopping list. We must therefore understand that prayer is a communication wholly different from speaking to our friends or even our pets. Prayer is an effort to communicate with a *higher* realm of our own being—a level of wisdom, love, purpose, and subtlety that is unquestionably transcendent. We must shift psychological gears to reach this level. We must also take the initiative to seek it. It is not seeking us out, although it may seem that way.

We best prepare ourself for effective prayer by establishing a state of mind that is calm and centered. From this quiet place within us, we need to attune to higher conscious forces through the right attitude, right expectation, and right intention.

This is why a thorough comprehension of what God is telling us in the 23rd Psalm is so essential. As we come to understand the special meaning of the symbols and meaning of this psalm, we are preparing ourself with the right attitude, right expectation, and right intention. The study of the messages and the qualities invoked in each part of this psalm helps prepare us for this attunement.

Armed with these insights, we are then better prepared to have a meaningful interaction with our spiritual contacts in times of prayer and contemplation.

For this reason, we need to recite the 23rd Psalm slowly and thoughtfully, taking time to ponder on the special meaning for us in each stanza. The idea is to begin with whatever understanding we have and then go beyond that to deeper insights. We begin with whatever peace or love we have in our hearts, and seek to deepen them as we contemplate the goodness of our divine possibilities. We may begin with words, but we must end with a deep comprehension. We may begin with a feeling of goodwill and peace, but we need to end with a sense of communion with something infinitely benevolent. We may begin with the belief that we are children of God, but we must end with an experience of our beingness in the life of God. This is the shift of consciousness that makes the power and promise of God—and the 23rd Psalm—come alive as a living presence in us. The words are no longer merely words—they are divine thunderbolts of benevolence and light!

At a more mundane level, we must never neglect the simple power of divine energies to repel and neutralize all manner of negative thoughts and feelings within us. Eventually we come to accept the fact that many of our worst enemies are within us, in the form of persistent doubts, fears, remorse, guilt, resentments, and limiting beliefs. The proper use of the forces and insights invoked through this psalm helps to heal these factors. As we figuratively hold up our fears and resentments and other negative qualities to the light, they begin to dissolve in this spiritual light.

So also, the same forces work to enrich the qualities of our thought, feeling, and intention. Half the time our problems are due to a critical lack of love to forgive, joy to persist in difficult times, power to endure in the face of opposition, and self-control to stay with a task until it is complete. The forces invoked in this psalm can supply what has been missing.

Eventually, our work with the forces invoked by the 23rd Psalm can serve to lift up our very sense of who we are. At first we come to a new and more refined vision of our divine possibilities. Then we discover a new and more noble vision of ourself and our relation to the Creator, our past, our future, and everything else involved in our life. As our awareness and conscious-ness expands, we move to a higher level of beingness—we become a new person in the light and love of God. This transformation makes all things about and in us new.

In this way, we move from healing and repairing our problems and wounds to genuine growth of character. And we can move even further still—to progressive stages of enlightenment that help us appreciate that we have always dwelt within the household of divine conscious-ness. This is our origin. This is our heritage. This is our destiny. This is our true home.

Fear No Evil

Part Three

Chapter 12

THE INNER SIDE
OF THE 23rd PSALM

The most powerful use of the 23rd Psalm involves the invocation and direction of the actual energies of spiritual qualities. If we can conceive that our love, joy, and knowledge are also forms of dynamic energies, then it becomes possible to relate to more than the idea and feeling of love or joy. We can also connect with the vital power of love, joy, and other qualities of the spirit. This is more than a semantic distinction. It is a breakthrough to the most powerful and dynamic way to pray and work with higher power.

If we are to work efficiently with these energies, we must understand a few simple concepts about how the energy field of our thoughts is organized. We all have a part of our personality that is able to think, organize, and solve problems. A different part of the personality deals with our emotional likes and dislikes, wants and wishes. Another part of us relates to other people and our need for support, approval, and encouragement. Still other parts enable us to express authority, discernment, survival, and a sense of identity. The *operation* of each of these major parts or divisions of our personality is related to a specific "force center" or center of energy in our thought field.

There are seven traditional energy centers in our "inner anatomy." These are:

1. **The base of spine** is the center for our *basic survival needs* and the functioning of both the body and the personality.

2. **The sacral area** is the center for *basic sustenance and self-expression.* It is the primary center for personal relationships, the expression of our personal control and our need for approval, support, and encouragement.

3. **The solar plexus** is the center for our *personal emotions*, ideals, desires, frustrations, and attachments.

4. **The heart center** serves to *center* our life essence, and gives us a sense of identity with our soul (the core of our character values and qualities) and "the heart" of groups to which we belong.

5. **The throat center** regulates *intelligent activity,* organization, and genuine creative self-expression (not imitative "creativity").

6. **The forehead center** is the seat of *discernment and integration* for our mind and heart, as well as the integration of personality and spirit.

7. **The top of head** is the center of our sense of *authority* and our impelling will-to-life.

We can compare the use of force centers to the way we store, prepare, and use food in our homes. We have special places to store different kinds of food. The fresh vegetables go into the refrigerator. The frozen meat and vegetables go into the freezer section. Canned items go into the cabinets. Flour and sugar go into special containers. Our meals are prepared on counter tops and in sinks, toasters, stoves, and microwaves. As we buy new groceries, therefore, we have a specific place to store them until we use them, places to prepare our meals, and still other places to sit and consume what we have prepared.

In a similar manner, when we invoke and receive new supplies of high quality "spiritual food"—such as love, joy, courage, insight, and tolerance—our inner self already has a specific system to sort out and integrate this new nourishment. New knowledge goes to the throat center. Love and forgiveness go to the heart and solar plexus centers. Reassurance, friendliness, hope, and charity go to the sacral center. New insights and beliefs go to the center in our forehead. New commitments and intentions go to the centers at the top of the head and to the throat.

The practical importance of these force centers is that our knowledge of them makes it possible to link and integrate the spiritual forces to our personality more efficiently. The end result is the *intelligent use of spiritual love and wisdom*.

The key to using the 23rd Psalm in connection with

these force centers lies in comprehending four basic ideas:

1. Each phrase of the psalm invokes a specific type of spiritual power—courage, faith, forgiveness, and the power to comfort.

2. This power can be directed to the appropriate energy center.

3. The purifying and energizing power of this quality is thereby directed more efficiently to heal and renew the personality.

4. We can set up triangles of circulating force among the force centers which will accelerate the integration of this new life of spirit into our character.

The specific formula for linking the key quality invoked by each phrase in the 23rd Psalm is listed in the tables below. For the sake of brevity, some of the phrases have been shortened from their original form. In practice, however, we would mentally recite the whole phrase with *a gentle mindfulness and appreciation of its inner meaning.* If recited slowly, there will be sufficient time to invoke and experience the energy of the key quality that comes with each phrase.

If working in this way is a new experience, it may be useful to imagine that you are centering your attention and "silent voice" at the level of the appropriate center. For best results, imagine that the energy is coming into your physical form from *behind* your spine for the centers at the base of the spine, sacral, solar plexus, heart and throat areas. For the center at the top of your head, imagine that the energy is coming from *above* and moving downward into it. For the center at the forehead, imagine energy coming *toward* your forehead. As you silently speak each phrase, just dwell on your best understanding of the meaning and quality of it. Let your creative imagination do the rest.

The specific correlations between the qualities invoked by each phrase and the proper center to direct it toward are as follows:

PHRASE	CENTER	QUALITY
Lord is shepherd	top of head	our power to live
I shall not want	base of spine	survival needs
lies down in green pastures	sacral	personal dignity, well-being, support
leads to quiet waters	solar plexus	serenity, dispassion, fulfillment
restores my soul	heart	core of character strength & identity
guides me in righteous paths	throat	intelligent choice and organization

This first section of the 23rd Psalm serves to build a bridge *from earth to heaven,* by opening us to higher possibilities. This attunement, however, does not happen automatically; it depends on our humble expectation and receptivity to higher power. The state of mind needed to make this invocation, or any prayer, effective is an amalgam of:

1. An unshakeable trust in higher power and its benevolence.

2. A positive expectation that we will be guided and enriched by this invocation.

3. A deep-seated gratitude for the blessings to be received.

4. A strong dedication to seek the highest and most noble of our human and divine possibilities.

When we prepare ourself in this manner, we are building a figurative bridge from earth—our personality—to heaven—our higher self or spirit. This bridge is built with our understanding, our faith, and the creative anticipation of a downpouring of new spiritual life from our higher self, the spiritual body within us.

Metaphorically, this is the part of the psalm where we are "breathing in" or invoking a divine blessing. The rest of the psalm will be concerned with the "breathing out" of this blessing—the qualities and insights we are seeking to receive—into the now receptive personality.

To continue the inner use of the 23rd Psalm:

PHRASE	CENTER	QUALITY
walk..valley of death I fear no evil	heart	power to protect, and preserve life
your rod and	sacral (later, the throat)	power to dispel evil and discipline self
your staff comfort me	solar	power to reward, heal, and enrich

Having made ourself receptive to higher power, we are now prepared to receive new healing life to protect and preserve our health and well-being. Note that the key phrase, "You are with me," implies the power of spirit brought down to our personal level—our heart—to help us. The "rod" is the symbol of higher power as the force which protects us from the "evil" of any threat to our well-being, dispels negativity, and disciplines our own immaturity. The "staff" is the symbol of higher power as the force which preserves the quality of our health and life and rewards right behavior.

These three qualities and energies and their corresponding centers form an important triangle of force—the *triangle of cleansing and renewal*. As we use our creative imagination to connect the heart and throat with the solar plexus, we also connect the purifying love and wisdom of our higher self with 1) our sense of identity, 2) our beliefs and convictions, and 3) our attitudes about our experiences. By resting in a mindfulness of this internal cleansing process we can allow the energies of this new life to move more fully into the mainstream of our beliefs and habits.

To continue the inner use of this psalm:

PHRASE	CENTER	QUALITY
Prepares a table	throat	gifts, treasures, and fruits of spirit
You anoint my head	forehead (representing top of head)	ability to receive a spiritual blessing
my cup overflows	heart	ability to accept this into heart and mind

The "table" is the wealth of spiritual treasures—wisdom, noble talents and qualities—we can receive when we are attuned to higher power. The "anointing" is a symbol of being blessed. The "cup" which overflows is our capacity to receive and retain new understanding, courage, and new degrees of compassion, joy, hope, and other fruits of the spirit. The "size of our cup" will depend on our willingness to give up our anger to make room for love, give up doubt to make room for faith, give up arrogance to make room for wisdom, and so on.

These three centers—the heart, the forehead, and the throat—form another triangle of energies—the *triangle of integration*. As you use your creative imagination to visualize energy circulating among them, this also connects the renewing and enriching power of spirit to our character to deepen our understanding and capacities for love of life, joy in living, perseverance, faith in our worth, optimism and all other fruits of the spirit.

To conclude our inner exploration of the energies of the 23rd Psalm:

PHRASE	CENTER	QUALITY
Surely goodness	heart	charity, goodwill
and love (mercy)	heart	forgiveness, tolerance, acceptance
dwell house of Lord	heart	power to reward, heal and enrich

This part of the psalm invokes a general blessing on our personality from the essences of our higher self. The work of the personality in this segment is to deepen its realization of the presence of this power, love, and intelligence. We need to *experience,* not just believe, the benevolent authority of our creative and divine essence and its ability serve as a source of constant guidance, love, and power to protect and preserve the best within our life. By using our creative visualization and mindfulness, we can circulate the energies of these key qualities and integrate them into the mainstream of our values and beliefs.

Our true goal in this phase of praying is to build our awareness that spirit can be an intimate part of all that we think and do. Since our spirit is benevolent, it will follow us—that is, support our worthwhile endeavors—wherever we go. And so, by extension, its goodness—its charity and loving-kindness—will "follow us" in whatever we do.

Likewise, our spirit is totally wise, and is aware of all of our activities and needs. Because it is benevolent as well, it views our indiscretions and mistakes with goodwill and an understanding of our long-range struggle to learn. Our Creator is a generous and concerned parent, who is determined to guide and discipline us wisely, forcefully, and kindly—although not indulgently. It is in this sense that mercy—God's compassion—will "follow us" in whatever we do.

As we commit ourself to live by these values and intentions, we shift our conscious experience and expression to a higher level. The goal is to *think and live as a spiritual person*, rather than as a primarily earthbound individual who is often self-centered and immature.

The "house of the Lord" is the poetic name for the enlightened state of consciousness of our spiritual body—

the Kingdom of Heaven within us. By the progressive realization of our divine potential and status, we do come to "dwell" in the enlightened state of wisdom, compassion, joy, talents, and courage that is our innate design for wholeness.

Putting It All to Work

The great destroyer of spiritual principles and practices is to reduce them to rigid rules and narrow expectations. Nowhere is this warning more relevant than when it comes to working with the subtle energies of love, joy, hope, faith, insight, or dedication. *While God remains impersonal and constant, our direct experience of divine qualities will always be subjective and personal.* Each effort to explore and deepen our understanding of these qualities can readily produce slightly different results and—sometimes—no apparent results at all. This is because our state of attention, mind, mood, receptivity, and capacity to absorb new things can vary. Our experience with divine energies of wisdom, serenity, joy, love, and forgiveness can also vary from day to day.

Therefore, instead of concrete expectations, the use of the 23rd Psalm to explore the inner dynamics of prayer and healing is meant to be *an experiment* each time it is tried. The proper attitude is one of intelligent curiosity and the quiet confidence that every sincere effort to work with higher power will be an enriching experience. We must be ready to accept the possibility that we might get no immediate results.

The effective use of prayer—and also meditation and contemplation—is similar to the results of an exercise program; the main benefits evolve from long term and persistent use. The same principle and effort in meditation can powerfully transform the quality of our beliefs and values. Therefore, sincere aspirants must be able to take a long range view of their efforts.

In summary, the primary benefits of the use of the 23rd Psalm, along with many other types of prayer and effective meditation techniques, is to deepen our conviction that there truly is a great benevolent power in and about us.

This power is *intelligent* and understands our needs and our path towards spiritual wholeness; it can be depended on to guide us. This power is *compassionate*, kind, and generous, but not indulgent or permissive; it can be depended on to support all our worthwhile endeavors. This power is *transcendent* of all earthly conditions; it can be depended on to be greater than any suffering, illness, or apparent obstacle we face.

Our duty is to do more than merely accept the possibility of a benevolent and generous nature of our Creator. We also need to do more than believe that it dwells within us as the very essence of our individuality and power to express ourselves. Our obligation is to comprehend and bring into manifestation this spiritual design for greatness as an enlightened character and noble lifestyle.

If we use the 23rd Psalm to pursue these goals, we will find that this psalm is an extremely powerful tool for our growth and enlightened mastery of self and the phenomena of life.

About The Author

Robert R. Leichtman, M.D. is one of the world's leading authorities on prayer and meditation. Born in Iowa, he graduated from the universities of Iowa and Michigan in the 1950's. He was in the private practice of internal medicine from 1962 to 1969, when his interest in the spiritual dimensions of life caused him to close his practice and devote his life to spiritual teaching, counseling, healing, and writing.

Since 1976, he has been a weekly participant in the spiritual healing services at the Mt. Washington Methodist Church in Baltimore that were begun by Olga and Ambrose Worrall in 1952. Dr. Leichtman is also an ordained minister in the Church of Religious Science.

Dr. Leichtman is the developer of Active Meditation, a meditative program suited for the Western aspirant, as well as numerous other classes. He has taught and lectured throughout the world.

In addition to *Fear No Evil,* he is the author of a six-book series on creativity, genius, and spirituality called *From Heaven to Earth.* The individual titles in the series are *The Psychic Perspective, The Inner Side of Life, The Hidden Side of Science, The Priests of God, The Dynamics of Creativity,* and *The Destiny of America.*

He is also co-author of *Active Meditation, Forces of the Zodiac, The Art of Living, The Life of Spirit, I Ching on Line,* and *Enlightenment.*

Other Books From Ariel Press

Additional copies of *Fear No Evil* are available at your favorite bookstore, or directly from the publisher, Ariel Press. To order from the publisher, please send $9.95 for each copy, plus $3 for postage. Send check or money order in U.S. funds to Ariel Press, 4255 Trotter's Way, #13-A, Alpharetta, GA 30004. Or call toll free at 1-800-336-7769 and charge the order to MasterCard, VISA, Discover, American Express, or Diners. In Georgia, add 6% sales tax.

Other books published by Ariel Press are also available, either at your local bookstore or from the publisher. Some of these titles include:

THE PSYCHIC PERSPECTIVE
by Robert R. Leichtman, M.D.
$11.95

THE INNER SIDE OF LIFE
by Robert R. Leichtman, M.D.
$11.95

THE HIDDEN SIDE OF SCIENCE
by Robert R. Leichtman, M.D.
$11.95

THE PRIESTS OF GOD
by Robert R. Leichtman, M.D.
$13.95

ACTIVE MEDITATION
by Robert R. Leichtman, M.D. & Carl Japikse
$19.95

MAKING PRAYER WORK
by Robert R. Leichtman, M.D. & Carl Japikse
$9.95

OUR SPIRITUAL RESOURCES
by Robert R. Leichtman, M.D. & Carl Japikse
$10.95

THE ART OF LIVING—5 VOLUMES
by Robert R. Leichtman, M.D. & Carl Japikse
$40

THE LIFE OF SPIRIT—3 VOLUMES
by Robert R. Leichtman, M.D. & Carl Japikse
$30

FORCES OF THE ZODIAC
by Robert R. Leichtman, M.D. & Carl Japikse
$19.95

I CHING ON LINE—4 VOLUMES
by Robert R. Leichtman, M.D. & Carl Japikse
$30

THE GIFT OF HEALING
by Ambrose & Olga Worrall
$7.95

EXPLORE YOUR PSYCHIC WORLD
by Ambrose & Olga Worrall
$7.95

PRACTICAL MYSTICISM
by Evelyn Underhill
$9.95

THE MYSTIC WAY
by Evelyn Underhill
$12.95

THE LIGHT WITHIN US
by Carl Japikse
$9.95

EXPLORING THE TAROT
by Carl Japikse
$14.95